中学英语教学设计与案例分析

ZHONGXUE YINGYU JIAOXUE SHEJI YU ANLI FENXI

主 编◎魏 惠

苏州大学出版社
Soochow University Press

图书在版编目(CIP)数据

中学英语教学设计与案例分析 / 魏惠主编. —苏州：苏州大学出版社，2017.3(2023.12 重印)
(基础教育改革与发展丛书. 第二辑)
ISBN 978-7-5672-2070-6

Ⅰ.①中… Ⅱ.①魏… Ⅲ.①英语课－教学设计－中学 Ⅳ.①G633.412

中国版本图书馆 CIP 数据核字(2017)第 051044 号

书　　名　**中学英语教学设计与案例分析**
主　　编　魏　惠
责任编辑　金莉莉
出版发行　苏州大学出版社
(地址：苏州市十梓街 1 号　邮编：215006)
印　　刷　镇江文苑制版印刷有限责任公司
开　　本　700 mm×1 000 mm　1/16
字　　数　189 千
印　　张　11.5
版　　次　2017 年 4 月第 1 版
2023 年 12 月第 9 次印刷
书　　号　ISBN 978-7-5672-2070-6
定　　价　36.00 元

苏州大学出版社网址　http://www.sudapress.com

总　序

目前，我国正处在从人力资源大国向人力资源强国、从教育大国向教育强国迈进的关键时期，在这特殊的历史阶段，基础教育正面临着一系列重大变革，需要我们用智慧去研究新情况、解决新问题，去创新我们的办学模式、教育模式和教育方法。淮阴师范学院长期坚持服务基础教育的办学理念，形成了鲜明的教师教育办学特色，在办学过程中，与区域中小学以及教育主管部门建立了亲密的战略合作伙伴关系，与基础教育之间建立了一种卓有成效的对话机制，注重在对话中发现问题，并提出解决问题的途径，取得了颇为丰硕的基础教育研究成果，在传承地方优秀教育理念、引领地方基础教育观念更新、推动地方教育与改革发展等方面做出了自身应有的贡献，成为区域基础教育改革与发展的直接参与者与有力推进者。

在这一背景下形成的《基础教育改革与发展丛书》（以下简称《丛书》）既是对该校近年来基础教育研究成果的总结，又是对当地基础教育改革发展的基本走向以及高等师范院校如何更好服务和引领基础教育改革与发展的战略思考。

《丛书》分三辑出版。第一辑为论文汇编，主要涵盖语文、数学、外语、物理、化学、生物、思想政治等学科的课程与教学研究，带有基础性和综合性的课程教学原理研究以及教育管理理论与实践研究。第二辑为专题研究，内容立足当前基础教育和教师教育改革与发展的热点和难点问题，深入、集中研究其中具有重大理论价值和重要实践指导意义的相关问题。第三辑为专著，主要围绕学科教学和基础教育改革与发展中的具有前瞻性、前沿性的深层次理论和实践问题，探索教育教学基本规律。

《丛书》突出彰显了以下几个方面的特点：

《丛书》是淮阴师范学院致力于更新基础教育理念和教师教育观念、引领地方基础教育发展、传承先进教育文化的产物。近年来，我国基础教育改革风起云涌,基础教育理念持续更新,新理念、新观念层出不穷;与之相对应,基础教育师资培养模式等也在持续变革,教师教育观念不断更新,教师教育体系在探索中持续重构。《丛书》体现了淮阴师范学院在基础教育理念和教师教育观念方面所进行的持续探索与努力,必将在推动基础教育改革与发展方面发挥重要作用。

《丛书》是淮阴师范学院从事教师教育的教师们教学相长的产物。书中的研究成果是他们长期思考与实践的结晶,同时《丛书》的编写对其专业成长必然发挥重要的促进作用。通过参与教育科学研究以及《丛书》的编写,他们的专业研究水平得到了很大的提升,同时也对其他教师的专业发展起到积极的示范作用。

《丛书》是淮阴师范学院致力于开放办学的产物。首先,《丛书》的作者队伍包括了淮阴师范学院的在职教师,以及与之有长期合作研究关系的部分淮安市中小学的教师,《丛书》在很大程度上是大学从象牙塔走向社会变革的一线并与变革的实施者直接对话的结果。其次,丛书所涉及的领域,诸如教师素质提高、教师专业发展、义务教育均衡发展、课程资源开发利用、课堂教学改革创新等问题,皆来源于基础教育实践的教育教学改革和学校管理方面的现实问题。再者,《丛书》的研究成果来源于教育实践,是教育理论与教育实践不断融通的产物,它又必将回归教育实践,通过各种方式对基础教育改革与发展实践产生积极影响。

相信《丛书》的出版将在提升淮阴师范学院基础教育研究品位、扩大其社会贡献度与美誉度等方面发挥积极作用,同时也将为全国其他一直致力于和基础教育表里通融、互通共进的师范院校提供参考和增添信心,共同为促进基础教育改革的深化,从而促进整个教育水平的提高做出更大的贡献。

袁振国
2011年12月
于中国教育科学研究院

目　录
Contents

一、 Welcome to the unit 课型

在牛津初中英语教材中,Welcome to the unit 是每单元的教学导入环节。它的教学目标在于激发学生的兴趣。这一教学板块有很多让学生发挥个性的空间。在该类课的讲授中,教师要尽可能地提供学习空间,让不同的学生在学习过程中获得乐趣、满足感与成功感。

(一) Welcome to the unit 课型特点及设计要求

Welcome to the unit 板块中语言点、知识点不多,漫画和图片较多。作为该单元的引子,它是一条线的开头。整个单元的教学内容都在这条线的引导下进行补充、调整或改编。教师要善于结合实际教学需要,灵活地和有创造性地使用教材,对教材的内容、编排顺序、教学方法等方面进行适当的取舍或调整。

Welcome to the unit 课型中各种任务的设计,如视、听、说、讨论、表演等方式,可以使学生锻炼各方面的技能,很好地融入英语知识的学习过程中,使学生在听和说的训练中提高英语交际能力,从而牢固地掌握基础知识,达到灵活运用的地步。

需要注意的是,Welcome to the unit 课型中应尽可能多地设计趣味性的任务型活动,让学生可以"学在玩中,玩中取乐",不仅要扩大学生知识面,还要提高学生的学习兴趣,为本单元的学习做良好铺垫。

再者,该课型帮助学生磨砺意志、陶冶情操、拓展视野、丰富生活经历、开发思维能力、发展个性和提高人文素养。在 Welcome to the unit 课型中大量图片和情境创设的帮助下,教师可以对学生进行适时的情感教育。如讲授 8B Unit 5 Good manners 和 8B Unit 7 International charities 时,可以尝试很好的德育教育,如爱国主义教育、感恩教育、爱心教育和环保教育。

此外,Welcome to the unit 课型应该最大限度给予学生相关的背景知识,

让学生在英语课堂中不仅把英语作为一门语言，更作为一种文化来学习。如8A Unit 2 School life 的 Welcome to the unit 中，可以适当地讲解 American English 和 British English 的区别和由来等，补充英美国家不同习俗的有关内容，让学生了解英语国家的风土人情、传统习惯等。

最后，Welcome to the unit 是巩固和扩展词汇的最好课型。这一课型可以通过展示大量图片扩充词汇。如 7A Unit 6 Food and lifestyle 和 7B Unit 8 Pets，都可以很好地进行适当的拓展，让学生了解更多生活中常用的词汇，为学生的英语学习奠定更好的基础。

（二）Welcome to the unit教学设计案例分析

七上　Unit 2　Let's play sports!

Comic strip and welcome to the unit

Background：Sports

It is important and fun for students to play sports and enjoy themselves.

Key words：Sports

Ⅰ　Background information

Nowadays, doing sports is very popular and they are good for our health. Also they can cultivate some good mental qualities, such as bravery, confidence. Besides, team spirit and cooperation can be reflected and improved. All these mental qualities are important for middle school students, which makes sports important for our students.

Ⅱ　Type of the lesson

Welcome to the unit

Ⅲ　Teaching aims and learning objectives

By the end of the lesson, the students will be able to:

1. Understand the meanings of the new words.

   Express the names of different sports in proper situations.

2. Instruct students to talk about their favorite sports.

3. Arouse students' interest in this unit.

4. Cooperate with partners and experience the feeling of success.

Ⅳ Teaching content

1. New words and expressions

2. The fun in sports

3. Learn with fun

Ⅴ Focus of the lesson and predicted area of difficulty

1. New words and expressions about sports

2. How to lead students to discuss more sports

3. How to improve students' involvement in class

Ⅵ Teaching aids

1. Multimedia 2. Blackboard

Ⅶ Teaching procedures

Step 1 *Different sports* (*Warm-up and lead-in*)

(1) Play a video and enjoy some pictures about different sports.

【设计理念：1. 观看近期内发生的或即将发生的体育事件视频，导入运动这一话题，给学生提供一定的背景知识，让学生对各种体育运动有一个直观的了解，引起学生对这一话题的兴趣。2. 用师生对话活跃课堂气氛，带领学生从沉闷的课堂一下子进入多彩的运动天地，调动学生的参与积极性，让学生爱上运动，爱上用英语交谈。】

T：Boys and girls, just now we watched a video of a recent sports event. Do you know what sports event it is?

Nanjing held the Youth Olympic Games in August, 2014. (Introduce the newest sports event to students.) This is an important sports event for teenagers around the world. During the Games, lots of teenagers from the world came to Nanjing to have competitions.

(2) Lead in the topic and some new words.

【设计理念：1. 通过视频中的截图，请学生辨认是哪种体育运动，让学生熟悉体育运动的名称。2. 通过图片导入生词(swimming, tennis, volleyball，板书并带读。扩充词汇 skating, shooting, table tennis, badminton，板书并带读)。】

T：There are many different sports in the Youth Olympic Games. I will show you some pictures.

Tell the names of the sports.

(3) Play a guessing game.

【设计理念：1. 通过你来描述我来猜的游戏，活跃课堂的气氛，调动学生参与课堂的积极性。2. 通过猜谜游戏，加深对运动词汇的熟悉和记忆。3. 促进学生用英语描述运动的能力。】

One of the students comes to the front and tries to describe some sports in English. Body languages are also allowed. The other students try to tell the names of the sports as soon as possible.

Step 2 *Sports*

(4) Presentation—favourite sports.

【设计理念：1. 通过三段小视频，让学生熟悉谈论爱好的短语和句型。2. 增加相关背景知识点的同时导入生词 enjoy，板书并带读。】

T: When you watch the videos, can you guess what their favourite sports are?

What is Sun Yang good at? (be good at)

What does Li Na love doing? (love doing sth.)

What does Messi enjoy doing? (enjoy doing sth.)

What do I like doing? (favourite, like sth. best)

(5) Complete the sentences in Part A on Page 19.

(6) Quick ask and answe: What is your favourite sport?

【设计理念：通过快问快答“你最喜欢的运动”这一形式使得学生很好地融入这一话题，鼓励学生用已学的单词和短语讨论他们的喜好，从而达到操练短语句型的目的。】

T: What sport do you like doing?

What sport do you love?

What sport do you enjoy doing?

What's your favourite sport?

What sport do you like best?

(Ask some of the students in class one by one.)

Step 3 *Talking about favourite sports*

(7) Listen and answer.

【设计理念：1. 播放书本上 Amy 和 Simon 的对话听力，再设计三个关于主旨大意的问题，让学生听懂关于最喜爱的运动的讨论。2. 通过问答反映学生是否听懂运动的内容，了解 Amy 和 Simon 两个人各自喜欢的运动，以及做运动的频率。】

T: Amy and Simon are talking about sports. Listen to their conversation and answer the following questions:

1) What sport does Amy like doing?

2) How often does Amy do it?

3) When does Simon play football?

(8) Read the conversation after the tape.

【设计理念：通过跟读，鼓励学生模仿对话的语音、语调，为接下来的环节即 pair work 做铺垫。】

(9) Pair work.

【设计理念：1. 从刚刚 Amy 和 Simon 的对话讨论这两人各自喜欢的运动以及锻炼的频率，过渡到班级学生喜欢什么样的运动以及运动的频率。让学生相互讨论，了解彼此的业余生活。2. 通过对话操练以及灵活运用询问爱好的短语和句型。】

Work in pairs and talk about your favourite sport.

A: I like …

What's your favourite sport … ?

B: I like …

A: Do you often … ?

B: Yes …

What about you?

How often do you … ?

A: …

Step 4 *Comic strip*

【设计理念：1. 通过播放 Eddie 和 Hobo 的视频，让学生熟悉 Eddie 和 Hobo 的对话，调动学生对话题的兴趣。2. 再次播放视频，鼓励学生模仿对话的语音、语调，并且分角色扮演，感受到英语的乐趣，寓教于乐。】

(10) Guessing.

T: Look at this picture. What's in Hobo's hands? He has a football in his hands. I think he likes football very much. Do you think so? What about Eddie? What is his favourite sport?

(11) Watch and answer.

T: What sport does Eddie like?

1) Read the dialogue after the tape.

2) Read the dialogue in roles.

3) Act out Eddie and Hobo's dialogue.

Step 5 *Homework*

【设计理念：1. 巩固今天所学内容。2. 鼓励学生查阅资料，对运动产生兴趣，并能在课余时间多做运动。】

T: Now please remember your homework:

1) Remember the words and phrases we have learned today.

2) Search more information about sports.

Ⅷ Blackboard design

7A Unit 2 Let's play sports!

Welcome to the unit

be good at love doing sth. enjoy doing sth. favourite, like sth. best	basketball, football, swimming, skating, shooting, running, table tennis, badminton

Ⅸ Teaching reflection

本节课的话题是运动，虽然比较贴近学生的生活，但是通常情况下男生对运动的话题更感兴趣，大多数女生对运动没有什么兴趣，因此要想上好这一课，必须让学生深入地了解多姿多彩、丰富多样的运动项目，我们为什么要做户外运动，以及户外运动可以为我们带来哪些乐趣等。这节课先从一个近期的大型体育事件入手，进行师生对话，让学生感受到体育运动的气势。然后一步步引导他们了解运动项目，并说一说三位体育明星喜爱和擅长的运动。紧接着通过 Amy 和 Simon 的对话让学生谈谈自己喜爱的运动以及平时做这项运动的频率，然后通过 Eddie 和 Hobo 的对话让学生体会运动是很有必要、很有益处的，再进行主题的升华，教会学生体验运动的乐趣。

这节课优点在于整节课主线明确，环节与环节之间有过渡。缺点在于：1. 操练这一环做得还不够充分，以及最后主题是直接升华，如果学生能从讨论中自己得出运动使我们受益，我们应该坚持运动的结论，那将更好。2. 在呈现运动形式和讨论最喜欢的运动环节，内容过于简单，有些活动设计有重复，可以再精炼一些，取其精华去其糟粕。3. 加强说的训练。4. 整节课稍显沉闷，可以多设计一些有趣的环节，增加课堂的趣味性。5. 在板书设计一块，可以有更多形式的变化。

点评：

本节课活动设计丰富多彩，首先视频导入，一开始就吸引了学生的注意力，引起了学生对运动这一话题的兴趣，并且与时事相关联，能够帮助学生增长知识。之后采取的 guessing game 的活动形式能够进一步调动学生参与课堂的积极性，并有效操练导入的生词。多次两人合作和小组合作形式也能够帮助学生及时进行操练，真正做到学以致用，过程中也不断培养了学生的合作能力和合作意识。本课尤其注重对学生口语的锻炼，例如，在处理连环画视频观看的环节中增加了学生跟读模仿的环节，能够有效地通过模仿的形式纠正学生口语的错误，并掌握地道的英语发音。综上所述，本课通过丰富多彩的活动和多样的设计很有效地调动起了学生的学习积极性，使学生对于本单元即将学习的内容充满了期待，但是也没有流于形式，过程中学生各个方面的能力也得到了充分的锻炼，真正地实现了生动而有效的课堂。在情感教育方面，通过对各种体育项目的生动介绍和与同伴之间的讨论，学生在无形中对体育运动有种跃跃欲试的心情，这个时候对于主题的升华就显得恰到好处，而不是流于简单枯燥的说教。

然而，美中不足的是本课过于坚守书本这一块阵地，仅仅拘泥于书本的内容，没能抓住某一个方面进行扩充。实际上，关于运动的话题，学生并不陌生，也比较感兴趣，可以适当扩展的地方也不在少数，如果本课在设计的时候能够以课本为基本导向，并跳出课本，打破常规的教学模式，打开思路，多补充一些课外知识，增加一些更加有新意的活动，可以为学生提供一个新的视野，打开新的思路。

七下 Unit 6 Outdoor fun

Comic strip and welcome to the unit

Background: Outdoor fun

It is fun for students to take part in outdoor activities and enjoy themselves.

Key words: indoor activities, outdoor activities, outdoor fun

Ⅰ Background information

At present, outdoor activities are quite popular in Western countries. They are good for our health. Also, they can cultivate some good mental qualities, such as bravery, confidence. Besides, team spirit and cooperation can be reflected and improved. Last but not least, it is important for students in middle school to learn with fun.

Ⅱ Type of the lesson

Welcome to the unit

Ⅲ Teaching aims and learning objectives

By the end of the lesson, the students will be able to:

1. Understand the meanings of the new words.

   Express the names of different outdoor activities in proper situations.

2. Instruct students to talk about their favorite outdoor activities.
3. Arouse students' interest in this unit.
4. Cooperate with partners and experience the feeling of success.

Ⅳ Teaching content

1. New words and expressions
2. The fun in outdoor activities
3. Learn with fun

Ⅴ Focus of the lesson and predicted area of difficulty

1. New words and expressions about outdoor activities
2. How to lead students to discuss more outdoor activities
3. How to improve students' involvement in class

Ⅵ Teaching aids

1. Video 2. Pictures 3. Blackboard 4. Chalk

5. Computer 6. Multimedia 7. Projector

Ⅶ Teaching procedures

Step 1 *Indoor activities* (*Warm-up and lead-in*)

(1) Play a video and enjoy some pictures about indoor activities.

【设计理念：1. 师生自由对话，探讨周一到周五都在室内度过好不好；如果不好，如何改善这一现状，有哪些方式可以改善。然后过渡到户外运动。导入三个生词(complain, hurry up, outdoor)。2. 用师生对话活跃课堂气氛，带领学生从沉闷的课堂一下子进入多彩的户外世界，调动学生参与的积极性，让学生爱上户外运动，爱上用英语交谈。】

T: What do you often do from Monday to Friday?

What activities can you do inside the house?

Do you like to stay inside the house all week long? But if you stay inside for a long time, how will you feel? You must start to complain. (板书带读 complain)

Is it good to complain? Come on! Hurry up! (板书，带读 hurry up)

Let's go outside and enjoy outdoor fun. (板书，带读 outdoor)

(2) Comic strip

【设计理念：1. 通过播放 Eddie 和 Hobo 的视频，让学生熟悉 Eddie 和 Hobo 的对话，调动学生对对话中谈到的话题的兴趣。2. 再次播放视频，鼓励学生模仿对话的语音、语调，并且分角色扮演，感受英语的乐趣，寓教于乐。3. 通过激发学生对户外运动的向往，为接下来的环节即讨论 outdoor activities 做铺垫。】

T: Now our friends Eddie and Hobo are also doing an outdoor activities. Let's watch and see what happened to them.

T: Does Eddie like it? (找一个学生回答) What does it do? (要求学生一起回答)

T: What does Eddie ask Hobo to do for him? (找一个学生回答)

Read after the video.

Read in roles.

Read together.

Prepare and act it out.

Step 2 *Outdoor activities*

(1) Get familiar with the names of different outdoor activities.

【设计理念：1. 通过播放一个含有各种户外运动的视频，让学生对视频中出现的户外运动有一个直观的了解。2. 通过视频中的截图，请学生辨认是哪种户外运动，让学生熟悉户外活动，并且能够造简单的句子。3. 通过图片导入四个生词（camping，riding，skating，jogging）。】

T：What kind of outdoor activities do Eddie and Hobo do? Yes，they go camping.（板书，带读 camping）

Do you know other outdoor activities?（带读 outdoor activities）

T：Do you want to go jogging?（带读 jogging）Then what kind of place is good for jogging? And what do you need if you want to go jogging? Who will go jogging with you? What about other outdoor activities?

Play a short video and talk about the names of the outdoor activities.

How many activities do you see in the video?

What are they?（导入并带读生词 camping，riding，skating，jogging）

(2) Match the pictures with the correct names.

【设计理念：1. 通过教师一遍遍带读和解释，让学生会拼、会读所学生词。2. 通过连线反馈学生是否掌握名称，只要求学生掌握 camping，riding，skating 和 jogging 这几个词的中文意思。】

(3) Listen to the dialogue about outdoor activities.

【设计理念：1. 播放书本上 Daniel 和 Amy 的对话听力，再设计两个关于主旨大意的问题，让学生听懂关于骑马和野营的户外活动的讨论。2. 通过问答反映学生是否听懂户外活动的内容，了解 Daniel 和 Amy 两个人各自喜欢的户外运动以及喜欢的原因。】

T：Our friends Daniel and Amy are talking about outdoor activities. Listen to the dialogue and answer the two questions.

T：What outdoor activities would Amy like to try?（请一个学生回答）

What outdoor activities would Daniel like to try?（请一个学生回答）Then what outdoor activities would you like to try? Why?（请一个学生回答）

(4) Pair work：talk about outdoor activities.

【设计理念：1. 从刚刚 Daniel 和 Amy 的对话讨论这两人各自喜欢的户外

运动以及喜欢的原因，过渡到班级学生讨论喜欢什么样的户外运动以及为什么会喜欢这个户外运动。让学生相互讨论户外活动，了解互相的业余生活。2. 通过对话操练以及灵活运用“What outdoor activities would you like to try?”这一句型。】

T: Now work in pairs to talk about what outdoor activities your classmates would like to try.

A: What outdoor activities would you like to try?

B: I want to go …

A: Why?

B: I love … What about you?

A: I want to go …

B: What do you like … ?

A: I like …

Step 3 *Group work*

【设计理念：1. 在小组合作的基础上运用本节课所学的生词、词组和句型讨论户外运动，包括喜欢什么类型的户外运动以及为什么喜欢这项运动。2. 让学生在讨论中明白做户外运动前要做好哪些准备，以及户外运动的注意事项有哪些。3. 在相互讨论中爱上户外运动。4. 运用发言稿形式鼓励学生大胆发言，倡导更多学生爱上户外运动。】

T: Now boys and girls, would you like to try some outdoor activities? What kind of outdoor activities would you like to try? If you are a tourist guide, what will you say to your group members to attract them to join you? Work in groups and make a report.

Step 4 *Homework*

【设计理念：1. 在小组合作的基础上，开始查阅资料，巩固课堂所学。2. 引导学生对户外运动产生浓厚兴趣，对自己的发言稿进行润色。】

T: Now please remember your homework:

(1) Make the report by yourself and share with each other.

(2) Choose one of your favourite outdoor activities and make a report for it.

Ⅷ Blackboard design

7B Unit 6 Outdoor fun—Welcome to the unit & Comic strip

(1) New words (2) Sentence

outdoor		camping	
hurry up	outdoor	riding	What outdoor activities
outside	activities	skating	would you like to try?
complain		jogging	

Ⅸ Teaching reflection

户外运动是运动的一种延伸,种类多样,精彩绝伦。要想上好这一课,必须让学生深入地了解什么是户外运动,户外运动包括哪些,我们为什么要做户外运动,以及户外运动可以为我们带来哪些乐趣等。这节课先从一个 free talk 入手,拉近师生距离,让他们感受到一直待在室内是多么的无趣。然后一步步引导他们可以去做做户外运动。再通过 Eddie 和 Hobo 的对话为接下来的关于户外运动的讨论做铺垫。接着播放一个户外运动的视频,进一步讨论各种户外运动。紧接着通过 Daniel 和 Amy 的对话让学生谈谈为什么要做户外运动,喜欢户外运动的理由是什么。然后进行主题的升华,教会学生体验户外运动的乐趣以及做户外运动时有哪些注意事项。

这节课优点在于整节课主线明确,环节与环节之间有过渡。缺点在于:1. 操练这一环做得还不够充分,以及最后主题是直接升华,如果学生能从讨论中得出这一主题那将更好。2. 播放过户外运动的视频之后可以问学生还知道哪些户外运动,扩大学生的词汇量,让学生在不知不觉中习得生词。3. 加强说的训练。4. 整节课稍显沉闷,可以多设计一些有趣的环节,增加课堂的趣味性。5. 在板书设计这一块,可以有更多形式的变化。

点评:

本节课是本单元的第一个板块,以激发学生兴趣为主,引入本单元话题,为本单元接下来的课程做好铺垫。要上好这个课型,教师必须设计丰富多彩的活动,充分调动学生的积极性,突出 Welcome 课型的趣味性。

本节课在设计上突出了语言的工具性特点,导入部分通过提问"What do you often do from Monday to Friday?"这样一个贴近学生生活的话题,激发并鼓励学生谈论喜爱的户外运动,通过鼓励孩子说来活跃课堂气氛。紧接着通过观看 Eddie 和 Hobo 的视频,激发学生对本单元的兴趣,通过两两对话及角色扮演熟悉对话内容,充分体现语言的交际功能。在表演时,鼓励学生模仿纯正的英语语音和语调,让学生在表演和对话中习得语言。接下来通过观看视频,了解更多的户外运动形式。观看视频是活跃课堂气氛、提高学生学习兴趣的一个重要途径。本节课通过将不同的户外运动形式融合在视频中,给学生营造一种欢乐的学习氛围,大大提高了课堂教学的有效性,相信学生在观看视频的时候,能更加深刻地记住不同的户外运动形式的英文表达方式。此外,本节课还通过两两合作及小组合作的形式,创造真实语言情境,让学生发挥自己的主观能动性,大胆地说英语,充分体现了语言的功能性。

然而本节课的设计也存在问题,最大的问题就是缺乏 Welcome 课型的趣味性。只通过观看 Eddie 和 Hobo 的对话以及户外活动介绍的一个视频还不足以充分调动学生的学习积极性。教师应多设计丰富多彩的活动,例如,组内猜词游戏(猜户外运动名称),小组之间有奖竞答游戏等,以增加 Welcome 课型的趣味性。

八上　Unit 4　Do it yourself

Comic strip and welcome to the unit

Background

Lots of students are very interested in DIY, and we can see DIY works everywhere in our life.

Key words: DIY, tools.

Ⅰ　Background information

Students want to do DIY jobs, but most of the time, they don't know how to do it well and they spend much money buying lots of materials instead of using the old things to do it.

Ⅱ　Type of the lesson

Welcome to the unit

Ⅲ　Teaching aims and learning objectives

By the end of the lesson, the students will be able to:

1. Understand the meanings of the new words.

   Use them in proper situations.

2. Know different functions of different tools.

3. Imagine how to repair the window when it is broken.

4. Cooperate with partners and experience the feeling of success.

5. Work in groups to make a DIY thing and then describe the steps of the DIY work.

Ⅳ Teaching content

1. New words: tool, repair, introduction, rope, scissors, exactly, decorate

2. Phrases: had better, get some tools, clear introductions
stand for, instead of, make some paper roses, a pair of scissors

3. Patterns: You'd better get some tools.

Ⅴ Focus of the lesson and predicted area of difficulty

1. Functions of the tools

2. Describe the steps of DIY work

Ⅵ Teaching aids

1. Blackboard　　2. Chalk　　3. Computer　　4. Multimedia

5. Some bottles and tools for DIY

Ⅶ Teaching procedures

Step 1 *Watch a video* (*Warm-up*)

Enjoy some pictures in the video about some very beautiful DIY works.

【设计理念：1. 通过教师制作的 video 导入 DIY 话题,吸引学生的注意力。video 里面的图片展示了很多精彩的 DIY 作品,也包括很多手工必需的工具和材料。】

T: Just now, we watched a video. What is the video about? Yes, it's about DIY. But what does DIY stand for? Yes, it stands for making, repairing and decorating things yourself instead of paying someone else to do it.

T: But before DIY, what should you do? Yes, you had better read the clear instructions very carefully, right?

Step 2 Lead-in (Talk to the students freely)

【设计理念：1. 通过自由对话的方式导入生词(词组)DIY, repair, decorate, stand for, clear instructions, had better 等。在语境中理解,学生更容易记得牢固。2. 强化学生对 DIY 的定义,激发学生的学习兴趣,调动参与的积极性。】

T：So boys and girls, do you like DIY? Me too! I even have a DIY box. Do you want to know what's in the box? Have a guess!

T：I have a pair of scissors, glue, tape and so on. And I also have this. What's this?

S：Hair clip.

T：Yes, I made it for my daughter. But you know, it's broken, so I have to repair it.

Step 3 *Make a birthday card*

【设计理念：1. 通过现场做生日卡片，让学生认知不同工具的使用及其功能，并且记住操作过程中使用到的工具。2. 让学生感知把普通的卡纸变成美丽的卡片的过程，从而增强他们自己动手的主观意识。3. 把卡片送给一位近期过生日的班级学生，让他体验老师的关怀。】

A：Make the card

T：But today I'm going to make something different. First, choose some colour paper like this, use the colour pen to draw some shapes on it, and cut it with a pair of scissors. When I cut it, I should be very careful because the scissors are dangerous, and I also need to be quick, because we don't have much time in class. Then use the tape or glue to stick it on another piece of color paper. After that, I can use something else to decorate it. At last, because it is a birthday card, what should I write?

S：Happy birthday!

T：Yes. Because Jack's birthday is coming, so let's give to him.

B：Know the tools and functions

T：What tools did I use when making the birthday card?

S：…

T：Yes. I show you the pictures and you tell me the name, OK?

Please read after me.

T：Now, all of you know the tools, but you know every tool has its function. Can you help me match the tools with their functions?

C：Pairwork (What can you do?)

T：Now, you know the names of the tools and all their functions. I want you to work with your partner. For example, I am a hammer. I can help ...

D: Guessing game (Who am I?)

T: You did a very good job. I'm very happy, so I want to play a game with you. But before the game, I want to tell you the rules. Rule 1, you don't have to put up your hands, just stand up as quickly as you can. Rule 2, please don't stand up when saying "one two begin". Rule 3, the most important one is that I have some presents for you if you guess it right.

Step 4 *Make paper roses (Part B: A talk between Suzy and Millie)*

【设计理念:1. 通过上一环节奖品 paper roses 导入到43 页 Suzy 和 Millie 的对话,通过提问三个问题,处理对话内容。2. 通过 pair work,让学生自由谈论感兴趣的 DIY,并说出制作该手工所需要的工具,强化学生对工具的认知。3. 通过提问"Who do you want to give it to?" 增强学生对父母、老师和朋友的感恩之心。】

A: A present from Suzy (Part B)

T: Just now, some of the students got some paper flowers from me. Do you like flowers? Suzy also likes flowers. Look at the picture. What kind of flowers are they?

S: Roses.

T: Yes, and because they are made of paper, so we call them paper roses. This time please turn your book to Page 43. There is a talk between Suzy and her friend Millie. Let's listen to it and answer 3 questions.

1. What do you do when you do DIY?
2. What is Suzy going to do?
3. What does Suzy need for her DIY?

B: Pair work

T: (请一个学生回答) Suzy wants to make paper roses. What about you? What tools do you need? Who do you want to give it to? Why? Different people may have different ideas. Now, please talk with your partner, and use the dialogue as a model.

A: *What do you want to make?* B: *I want to make ...*

A: *What tools do you need?* B: *I need ...*

A: *Who do you want to give it to?* B: *I want to give it to ...*

Step 5 *Comic strip*

【设计理念：1. 通过看 video、回答问题、带读、齐读等方式处理 Hobo 和 Eddie 的对话，让学生深入理解对话内容，感受漫画的幽默所在。2. 通过设计 Hobo 在 DIY 过程中犯的错误，让学生想办法弥补，让破掉的洞实用又美观，可以充分发挥学生的创造性和想象力。而这样的品质也是 DIY 时必须要具备的。3. 操练本节课重点句型：You'd better do sth. 。】

A：Comic strip

T：I know most of you are interested in DIY. What about our friends Hobo and Eddie? Are they interested in DIY? Now, please turn your book to Page 42. There is a dialogue between Hobo and Eddie. So let's watch the video and answer the three questions.

1) What does Eddie buy for Hobo?

2) What should Hobo do first?

3) Why can't Eddie help Hobo?

B：Who can help Hobo?

T：From the video, we can see that Eddie didn't want to help Hobo make the house, so he had to make it himself, but Hobo was so careless that he made a hole on the wall. Can you give Hobo some creative ideas to solve the problem? For example, you can make a window here. Now, you can talk to members in your group. You can use the sentence structure：

You'd better ________________________.

Step 6 *Group work：DIY a vase for Hobo.*

【设计理念：1. 发挥学生的创造性和自己动手的能力，同时引导学生学会废物利用，看似无用的瓶子经过精心的 DIY，都可能变成实用又美丽的花瓶，实现废物利用，避免浪费。2. 在小组活动中，分工明确，可以增强组内成员的团队合作精神，提高效率，同时体验成功。3. 在一节课内容学习之后，希望学生能通过组织语言，将本节课的重点进行语言输出。】

T：With your help, Hobo made the house successfully. But look at the picture, there is nothing in the house, so do you think it's beautiful?

S：No!

T: So I want you to make a vase for Hobo to make the house beautiful. But I don't have much money, so I give you some bottles, tools and some other materials. Please work in groups to make a vase and then you can choose one reporter to tell us how to make it, and choose one model to show us the vase. Then we will choose the most beautiful one for Hobo.

Dear Hobo,

We want to DIY a vase for you!

First, we ____________________ *Second, we* ____________________

Then, we ____________________ …

We hope you will like it and have fun in your new house!

T: All the vases are great. I think Hobo will be very happy to see that. Thank you!

T: Boys and girls, in today's lesson, we know that we can use our own hands to make lots of beautiful things, right? So next time, when you want to throw something away, please think about if we still can make use of it.

Step 7 *Homework*

【设计理念：1. 因为本节课的时间有限，在设计时 Hobo 和 Eddie 的对话部分没有要求学生表演，但是此部分学生仍很感兴趣，所以可以以小组的形式课后准备，下节课挑选部分小组表演。2. 希望学生能在能力范围内用自己的双手为父母送上礼物。】

T: Now please remember your homework:

1) Listen to the comic strip and act it out.

2) DIY something for your parents.

Ⅷ Blackboard design

8A Unit 4 Do it yourself——Welcome

DIY a birthday card	repair
You'd better	decorate
	clear instructions

Ⅸ Teaching reflection

本节课以 DIY 为主线，从对工具的认知到其对应的功能，再到手工作品的制作。总体而言,本节课充分调动了学生参与课堂的积极性和主动性,因为此话题是这一代学生非常熟悉的,随着时代的发展,他们的手工已经不仅仅局限于谋生,而是为了乐趣。本节课的设计更重要的一个出发点是希望学生多将身边闲着的废弃物进行手工改造,实现废物再利用。

从课堂的效果来看,有几个环节学生参与积极性较高。一部分就是 guessing game 环节,因为是抢答,又有礼物驱动,参与的热情很高涨。另外一个部分是教师现场制作的圣诞卡片,学生很有兴趣。还有最后 vase 的制作,小组活动气氛很浓厚。

但原本以为是亮点设计的帮助 Hobo 修房子部分,却因为学生的想象力没有完全被激发出来,而显得有些冷场。教师提前应该多给学生一些例子引导,不能让学生的思维局限在某一个方面,这也是以后需要深入思考的地方。

点评:

Welcome 课型包括两大部分:开篇的卡通画(Comic strip),风趣的漫画、简洁的对白,带着学生轻松地进入本单元的学习;导入(Welcome to the unit),一组图片、一段对话,激活学生关于本单元话题已有的知识和经验。因此,课堂中各种任务的设计应重在培养学生的学习兴趣,提高学生英语学习的积极性,使他们很好地融入英语知识的学习过程中。比如,本节课的授课老师设计了 guessing game 这一环节,既有抢答,又有礼物作为奖励,这使得学生能够更加积极地参与到活动之中。教师现场制作的圣诞卡片和最后 vase 的制作这两个环节设置非常巧妙,牢牢地吸引了学生的注意力,激发学生对英语课的兴趣,活跃了课堂气氛。试想这一年龄段的青少年谁不喜欢玩游戏和手工制作呢?

另外,通过各种有效的教学设计,使学生在听和说的训练中提高英语交际能力,从而牢固地掌握基础知识,达到灵活运用的地步。例如,授课教师由上一环节奖品 paper roses 导入到下一环节 43 页 Suzy 和 Millie 的对话,通过提问三个问题,处理对话内容,然后通过 pair work,让学生自由谈论感兴趣的 DIY,并说出制作该手工所需要的工具,强化学生对工具的认知。这一环节有助于学生将本堂课所学内容用于实际的英语交际当中,活学活用。

最后,本节课教师展示大量的图片和创建情境,对学生进行适时的情感教育。英语课程标准指出,英语课程的学习,既是学生通过英语学习和实践活动,逐步掌握英语知识和技能,提高语言实际运用能力的过程;又是他们磨砺意志、陶冶情操、拓展视野、丰富生活经历、开发思维能力、发展个性和提高人文素养的过程。授课老师非常细心,而且能够做到在恰当的时候对学生进行教育。比如,制作完 paper roses 后,教师通过提问"Who do you want to give it to?"增强学生对父母、老师和朋友的感恩之心。还有,Hobo 在 DIY 过程中犯了错误,老师鼓励学生想办法帮 Hobo 弥补,让破掉的洞实用又美观。这有助于孩子养成乐于帮助别人的美德。

八下 Unit 7 International charities

Comic strip and welcome to the unit

Background

Key words: charities around the world

Ⅰ Background information

At present, there are lots of people who are in need, such as people with serious diseases, blind and deaf people, children without families, people in poor areas, the elderly, earthquake survivors and so on. There are some international charities in the world and they do something to help people in need. It is important for students to cultivate some mental qualities by learning this lesson, such as kindness, be willing to help others and so on.

Ⅱ Type of the lesson

Welcome to the unit

Ⅲ Teaching aims and learning objectives

By the end of the lesson, the students will be able to:

1. Memorize the new words and phrases.
2. Learn some famous international charities.
3. Think about how to help the people in poor areas better.
4. Learn about the passive voice in the simple present tense.
5. Arouse students' interest in this unit.
6. Cooperate with partners and experience the feeling of success.

Ⅳ Teaching content

1. New words and phrases
2. Some famous international charities

Ⅴ Focus of the lesson and predicted area of difficulty

1. New words and phrases
2. Four international charities
3. Passive voice in the simple present tense
4. How to improve students' involvement in class

Ⅵ Teaching aids

1. Video 2. Pictures 3. Blackboard 4. Chalk
5. Computer 6. Multimedia 7. Projector

Ⅶ Teaching procedures

Before class, students listen to a song called "Tell me why".

【设计理念：课前播放英语歌曲"Tell me why"，表达了一个小男孩想要帮助世界上需要帮助的人们的心声，为本节课做了一个很好的铺垫，即及时为需要帮助的人们伸出援助之手。】

Step 1 *Warm-up and lead-in* (*about* 5 *mins.*)

【设计理念：从歌曲导入，师生自由对话，激发学生帮助他人的意识。通过一张世界地图向学生呈现世界上最富有的十大国家和最贫穷的十大国家来激发学生学习本课的兴趣，让学生思考如何帮助贫穷地区的人们，导入本课的话题 international charities。】

T: Do you like the song? Did you understand the song? What does the boy want to know?

S: ...

T: In the world, lots of people are in need. Look at the world map. What are the ten poorest countries?

S: They are ...

T: People in poor areas/countries don't have ... ? What do they need?

S: ...

T: How can we help them?

S: We must do something to help. We can donate money to them.

T: Have you ever done anything for charities? Were you happy to help charities?

S: ...

T: It's our duty to help them. There are many international charities in the world. What international charities do you know?

Step 2 *Presentation*

【设计理念：通过呈现四大国际慈善组织，让学生对它们的缩写、全称、标志、作用等有更加深入的了解。】

1) ORBIS

T: What does the signal look like? What kind of people does it help?

(Read a table to learn more about ORBIS. In the signal, we can see there is a plane. ORBIS uses a plane to visit poor areas. So it is called "Flying Eye Hospital". ORBIS helps blind people and people with eye problems.)

2) WWF

T: Its full name is World Wide Fund for Nature. Look at pictures. How does it help?

(It is an international charity to help protect the wild animals in the world.)

3) Oxfam

T: It helps people in poor countries.

Read a passage and learn about what Oxfam works for.

Look at pictures and learn about other Oxfam events.

4) UNICEF

T: It stands for United Nations Children's Fund. How does this charity work? Read Part B and answer the question. (It helps build a better world for everyone, especially children all over the world. It provides basic education for children in poor areas. It works for the equal rights of girls and women too. It also works to prevent the spread of some serious diseases, like AIDS, among young people.)

Step 3 *Guessing game*

【设计理念：通过这个活动来检查学生对四大慈善组织的记忆情况以及他们灵活运用所学知识的能力。在这个活动过后提出一个问题，问学生想为哪个慈善机构效力，既很好地承接了上文，又很自然地导入了下文，即 B 部分的对话。】

T: We have learnt four international charities. Now let's play a guessing game.

Look at part of the pictures and guess what kind of international charities it is.

Which charity can help them?

Problem 1: ______________________________

Some restaurants sell dishes made in rare animals which are protected by laws (法律).

Problem 2: ______________________________

Children in poor areas in Africa don't have enough food to eat or enough houses to be their shelters. They are ill, but they can't go to hospital. They are old enough, but they can't go to school.

Problem 3: ______________________________(Listen and fill in the blank)

Problem 4: ______________________________

Catherine has been blind since she was sixteen years old. Now ten years has passed, but she still can't see anything because she is very poor and hasn't got enough money to go to hospital.

T: Which charity would you like to work for? Why?

S: …

Step 4 *Presentation*

【设计理念：接上面的问题，如果有学生谈论到 UNICEF，那么将进一步阐释该慈善机构并板书带读 equal rights, basic education 和 especially，为 B 部分的对话做了很好的铺垫。同时将 B 部分的对话作为听力材料，很好地锻炼了学生的听力。】

T: (If the student says he would like to work for a charity called UNICEF.) Everyone has the equal rights to receive education. However, some children, especially those from poor areas, can't go to school like us. We should try to help them go back to school. (板书并带读 equal rights, basic education 和 especially)

Mr Wu is asking the students about international charities. Listen to the tape and tell me how UNICEF helps people.

S: …

T: Read the conversation after the tape. Pay attention to your pronunciation and intonation.

Step 5 *Comic strip*

【设计理念：通过回答问题让学生对漫画的内容有更深刻的理解；通过背诵并表演对话，让学生在忠于原文的基础上适当地加入自己的想象力从而丰富漫画的内容，让学生能在具体的情境中灵活运用英语；通过讲解知识点，让学生了解一般现在时的被动语态。】

T: Hobo wants to do something for charity.

Activity 1: Answer the questions: 1. What is needed for charity?

2. What does Hobo want Eddie to do?

3. What does Eddie want to do first? Why?

4. How far will they go?

Activity 2: Recite and act the dialogue out.

Activity 3: Language points

Step 6 *Group work*

【设计理念：通过这样一个大活动来创设真实的语境，旨在让学生之间用英语谈论如何帮助贫困地区的人们。】

Choose our chairperson

T: As we all know, helping others is helping ourselves. Do you want to do something to help others?

T: Here is an activity: Choose our chairperson.

Do you want to be a chairperson of one of the international charities? If you do, please make a speech in the class. Here are some tips for you:

Good morning, ladies and gentlemen,

- My name is ... I want to be a chairperson of the Oxfam/UNICEF/OBRIS ...
- If I can be the chairperson. I will try my best to ..., and ...
- So if you like me, please support me. At last, I want to thank ... for your help. Thank you very much.

T: We need more charities. We need more people to take part in charity work.

Step 7 *Homework*

【设计理念：1. 在小组合作的基础上，开始查阅资料，巩固课堂所学。2. 结合导航单，先学 Reading Ⅰ。】

T：Now please remember your homework：

1）Remember the new words and phrases.

2）Recite the dialogues.

3）Search more information about international charities on the Internet.

4）Preview reading.

Ⅷ Blackboard design

8B Unit 7 International charities

International charities
- ORBIS：to treat（治疗）eye problem in poor areas
- WWF：World Wide Fund for Nature
  to help protect the wild animals in the world
- Oxfam：help people in poor countries
- UNICEF：United Nations Children's Fund
  - to build a better world for everyone，especially children all over the world
  - to provide basic education for children in poor areas
  - to work for the equal rights of girls and women
  - to work to prevent the spread of some serious diseases，like AIDS，among young people

Ⅸ Teaching reflection

这节课先从一首歌曲"Tell me why"导入，为引入话题做了很好的铺垫。接着 free talk，拉近师生距离，唤起学生的善良意识，让他们觉得加入国际慈善组织是件很有意义的事。然后详细地介绍了四大国际慈善组织并且对此做了相关的 guessing game，形式丰富，既锻炼了学生解决实际问题的能力，也很好地考查了学生的掌握情况。然后通过 B 部分的对话，让学生听对话回答相关话题，锻炼了学生的听力。接着让学生回答漫画部分的对话，充分发挥想象力来表演漫画，培养了学生对英语学科的兴趣，通过讲解知识点，加深了学生对文本的理解，并且对被动语态有了一定的了解，为语法学习做了铺垫。最后通过一个大活动，让学生参与到帮助他人的队列，以演讲的形式就本节课的学习进行输出。这样就升华了本课的主题，让学生意识到帮助别人就是帮助自己,送人玫瑰,手有余香。

这节课优点在于整节课流程清晰,结构紧凑。缺点在于:1. 操练不够充分,如果能在大活动过后设计一些题目会使本课更加充实。2. 个别环节的串词不够流畅。3. 整节课稍显沉闷,可以多设计一些有趣的环节,增加课堂的趣味性。4. 板书待优化,增强设计性。

点评:

Welcome 课型旨在为学生简略介绍本单元所学内容,通过各环节的精心设计与活动的安排,激发学生的学习兴趣,提高学习的主观能动性,同时,也从单词、词汇和语法层面,让学生对于本单元有基本的认识与了解。

本节课环节设计紧凑,合理地体现了教学目标,能够帮助学生系统并详细地了解国际慈善组织的名称及各自的职能,并通过 guessing game 进行反馈,巩固学生的记忆。课堂任务的安排明确有效,层层递进,既能融入听、说、读、写等语言技能的训练,又能帮助学生更好地理解文本,更能培养学生解决实际问题的能力。课堂活动的安排则体现了教师"教"与学生"学"的统一。任务的抛出,给了学生提示,通过一个个活动的完成,教师最大限度地调动了学生的语言输出能力,让学生在不知不觉中学会了语言技能与知识。

Welcome 课型注重趣味性和实用性,国际慈善组织通过不同的方式帮助各种所需人群,通过相关视频的使用,并结合一些直观的图片,不仅能激发学生的兴趣,还能够在情感上引起学生的共鸣,并且学生情感上的认同能促使他们更多地了解四大慈善组织,从而提升学生的自主学习能力。group work 的设计让学生开动脑筋,集思广益,并利用课堂所学组织自己的语言,真正做到学以致用,本课的主旨也得到了升华。

当然,本节课在知识点操练方面还有待加强,板书的设计略显烦冗,需要改进。课堂活动可再做深度思考,让学生学会合作,加强讨论,取长补短,共同学习。

九上 Unit 2 Colours

Comic strip and welcome to the unit

Background: The rainbow

Teacher helps students to talk with each other about the colours of the rainbow.

Key words: rainbow, colours

Ⅰ Background information

A rainbow is a beautiful natural phenomenon. People will be amazed by its beauty, especially its surprising colours. Students in Grade 9 are very curious and they have the ability to talk about its seven different colours. Therefore, they must have a great interest in talking with their partner about colours.

Ⅱ Type of the lesson

Welcome to the unit

Ⅲ Teaching aims and learning objectives

By the end of the lesson, the students will be able to:

1. Understand the meanings of the new words.
   Use them in proper situations.
2. Review and grasp the seven colours of the rainbow and their order.
3. Talk about colours with their partners in English.
4. Experience the beauty that the nature brings to us.

Ⅳ Teaching content

1. New words
2. The colours of the rainbow
3. Comic strip

Ⅴ Focus of the lesson and predicted area of difficulty

1. New words and the sentence structure
2. How to describe colours
3. How to lead students to talk about colours with partners

Ⅵ Teaching aids

1. Blackboard 2. Chalk 3. Computer 4. Multimedia
5. Projector

Ⅶ Teaching procedures

Step 1 *Free talk and lead-in*

(1) Play a video about the Rainbow Colours Song to lead in the topic of colours.

T: Boys and girls, just now we watched a video. Do you know what it is about? Is it very beautiful? Do you like it very much?

【设计理念：1. 课前播放视频，能迅速激起学生的兴趣，引入话题。2. 颜色话题贴近生活实际。3. 在学生回答老师提问时，很自然地应用一些不同颜色的词汇，并带学生反复朗读。】

(2) Show several pictures and discuss the colours of the rainbow.

T: How many colours are there in it? What are they?

They are red, orange, yellow, green, blue, indigo, violet. Please read after me.

How do you feel about the colours of the rainbow? Are you very happy?

Do you have a better way to spell the words of the seven words?

【设计理念：在老师与学生的交流讨论中，有意识地引导学生关注彩虹的颜色，并掌握七种颜色词汇的朗读和拼写。】

Step 2 *Quick response*

T: OK. Let's have a game! I will show you some pictures, and you should quickly tell me the colour of each one, understand? Who is the fastest one?

Great! Please read after me.

"red, orange, yellow, green, blue, indigo, violet".

【设计理念：快速反应的形式，调动课堂气氛，同时也引入了本课的一些重要生词。在教学过程中，注重单词的拼写和音标教学以及四会单词的带读和拼读。】

Step 3 *Presentation*

T: Boys and girls, colours are everywhere, in our school, in our homes and so on. OK, I'll show you a video. Please watch the video and tell me how many colours there are in it.

What is it? Do you know how many colours there are in it?

In the video, which is your favourite colour? /Which colour do you like best?

Colours can make our life wonderful. We can't live without it. Amy and Shirely like colours, too.

【设计理念：多样化的教学呈现形式可以充分抓住学生的注意力，让学生在课堂上全神贯注。同时，学生的感官被充分调动，有效练习听说读，且呈现

方式由词汇到句型，逐层递进。通过观看视频中关于学校场景的细节，增强学生对学校的热爱之情，渗透情感教育。】

Step 4 *Part B & Pair work*

T: Now I will play a tape on the conversation between Amy and Shirley. Please listen to their conversation. While listening, you have to answer two questions.

1) How many colours are there in a rainbow?

2) What is Shirley's favourite colour? And why?

T: Open your book to Page 21 and then read their dialogue.

T: Boys and girls, which is your favourite colour? Please work in pairs and talk with your partner about colours. (找两组)

【设计理念：阅读课本 B 部分对话回答几个问题，并以此为模板，两人一组编对话，创设真实的情境，让学生谈论他们自己最喜爱的颜色，让学生能够运用所学的知识进行英语对话。

在此过程中，教师提供一些表达，如，A: Do you know how many colours there are in ... ? / Which is your favourite colour? Why? / I like ... best 等。鼓励学生多使用英语来讨论本单元的话题。】

Step 5 *Comic strip*

Watch and answer questions. Read after the video. Read in pairs. Act out the dialogue.

T: Look at the picture and answer two questions:

1) Which colour does Eddie want to wear, pink or blue?

2) Why does Eddie like this colour?

T: Read after the video. Read in pairs. Act out the dialogue.

【设计理念：让学生带着问题去观看视频。在跟读对话时，注重语音、语调的培养，提高学生的口语水平。以小组为单位，表演漫画，学生在这样的活动中兴趣高涨，充分体现新课程自主探究、合作交流的学习方式。老师在教室里巡视，及时给有困难的小组或学生提供帮助。】

Step 6 *Group work*

T: Boys and girls, colours are very important in our daily life. The world would be a dull place without colours. Do you want to study in a colourful classroom?

You can design your dream classroom, especially what the classroom is like, what the colours of the classroom are.

Work in groups and discuss with your group members.

【设计理念：在设计理想教室的情境中进行当堂反馈，让学生先在组内讨论再进行对话，能够扩大学生的参与面。在此过程中，学生可以发现颜色的美，用颜色来点缀生活。】

Step 7 *Conclusion*

Boys and girls, we are lucky enough to see so many colours. Please love life, and enjoy life. Every day is so colourful.

【设计理念：对学生进行热爱生活的情感教育。情感主题升华，让学生能再次体会颜色对生活的影响，热爱生活，享受生活。】

Step 8 *Homework*

T: Boys and girls, you all did a good job. Here is your homework:

1) Read and recite comic strip.

2) Preview reading.

3) Make a poster about your dream classroom.

【设计理念：学生完成课后作业并制作一张英文海报。通过这样的作业争取让每一个孩子将当堂所学知识加以应用。制作海报可以提高学生的学习兴趣，增强学生的创造性，激励全体学生努力学习。】

Ⅷ Blackboard design

9A Unit 2 Colours—Welcome to the unit

The rainbow

Ⅸ Teaching reflection

本课在设计时突出体现了 Welcome 课型激发学生学习兴趣的教学目标。用有趣的彩虹视频导入，使学生感到非常新奇，注意力被充分吸引到课堂上来。在教学过程中，同样引入了多种形式的呈现方式。多种形式的呈现方式与学生听、说、读、写能力的训练紧密结合，初步实现了寓教于乐的教学愿景。在素材的选取上，以贴近学生实际生活为原则，使学生兴趣盎然，教学氛围轻松愉悦。

教学流程按照由词到句、由句到篇的方式安排，层层递进，充分考虑学生的学习规律，帮助学生掌握新知。

课堂各项环节的设计都是基于小组的形式，运用了 pair work，group work 等活动，体现了“自主、合作、探究”的理念，突出了学生学习方式的转变，创设了互动、轻松、愉快、和谐的学习氛围，能有效地促进学生积极地参与学习过程。而小组合作互助学习建立在充分的先学基础上，突出了小组互助的力量，强调了学生的学在教学中的重要性。

但是，Welcome 课型内容少而简单，主要内容之一是介绍了彩虹的颜色，本课的重点就是简单地让学生掌握彩虹的颜色。在反思过程中，我发觉自己忽略了一点：彩虹属于雨后偶尔出现的美丽的自然景观。因此，我可以以此为突破口，带领学生去领略更多大自然的美丽景观。然后，以这些呈现的图片作为接下来的 pair work 素材。这要比 the Olympic rings，the playground 等更贴切，更符合实际。

此外，基础较弱的学生参与积极性不高。以后在备课中要多做预测，多思考如何设计活动，让全体学生都能最大限度地参与课堂，使活动更加精炼，课堂更加高效。

点评：

Welcome to the unit 这个板块是每一单元的第一课时，是一个引子，在这个板块里，语言点知识内容都不多，有漫画和图片，相对于本单元其他的板块，学习内容是比较轻松愉快的。因此，对本板块的设计要强调趣味性和引导性，在这方面，本课的设计还是比较到位的，课的开始就用彩虹视频引出本单元的话题颜色，使得学生在上课伊始，兴趣就被调动起来，积极投入英语课堂；同时，通过视频带领学生学习一些关于颜色的生词，实现了寓学于乐的良好效果。在之后的操作环节，运用 quick response 等具有竞争性的游戏策略，激起学生掌握知识的欲望，推动他们巩固已学知识。此外，本节课还基于 pair work 和 group work 等合作形式来设计课堂任务，使学生在听和说的训练中提高英语交际能力，从而牢固地掌握基础知识，达到灵活运用的地步，陶冶语言情操。在 act out 环节，给予学生充足时间自编自导，演出漫画内容，提高学生表达能力，活跃课堂气氛。在设计教学任务的时候，本课还注意以学生真实的生活环境为背景，引导学生关注自己教室、家的颜色设计，使得课堂不脱离生活；结束环节的升华设计，引导学生关注颜色带来的身心变化，提高学生的审美意识，陶冶情操，拓展视野，丰富生活经历，开发思维能力、发展个性和提高人文素养。

本课设计紧扣 Welcome 课型的趣味性，美中不足的是 Welcome 内容偏少，如果能适当给学生增加一些与颜色有关的阅读文章，拓展学生的知识面并充实课堂内容会更好。

二、 Reading Ⅰ课型

英语阅读教学是提高学生学习外语兴趣、积累语言知识的主要途径;通过阅读教学,学习者的能力不断提高,阅读的兴趣会从纯语言学习性阅读逐步发展到语言应用性阅读;从阅读入手是培养语感、积累语言经验的有效途径,文字材料是外语学习赖以进行的基础;不仅使英语学习者增长知识,提高兴趣,而且会提高其想象、概括、归纳综合、逻辑推理、理解记忆等综合能力。

(一)Reading Ⅰ课型特点及设计要求

阅读是语言学习过程中最重要的信息输入途径之一,是语言输出的基础。阅读是一个复杂的心理活动过程,阅读的过程不仅是要理解文字符号的表层结构,还要理解语义的深层结构的转化,是读者与文章之间互动的一种信息加工方式,是读者积极主动地在其语言知识及背景知识的参与下对文章的信息进行重新加工和构建的过程。初中英语阅读教学的目的是激发学生的阅读兴趣,教给学生阅读方法,训练其阅读技巧,从而扩大学生的词汇量,丰富语言知识,提高语言的运用能力,最终培养学生终身阅读的习惯。

以教材导入,开拓阅读视野;以视听入手,注重整体感知;以语篇推进,加强过程指导;以任务驱动,拓展文化外延。

英语阅读教学的实施分为三个基本阶段:阅读前(Pre-reading),阅读中(While-reading),阅读后(Post-reading)。

阅读前(Pre-reading)

这是阅读课的第一步骤,也是阅读的导入阶段,读前活动的教学策略在于激发兴趣,聚焦主题,即让学生对文章中的话题产生兴趣并能自然地过渡到目标文章的阅读当中,为要阅读的内容做好铺垫,提高阅读速度和质量。

1. 激发兴趣,让学生带着兴趣,带着动机去阅读,把学生的注意力集中到课文的语言情境中来，激发学生的阅读欲望。

2．激活和提供必要的背景知识，引出话题。让学生能够熟悉话题，熟悉他们所要读的内容，把文章的主题呈现给学生或引导学生对要阅读的内容做出预测。

3．为深入阅读扫清词汇的障碍以及做一些语言的准备。

常见的读前活动有问题导入、实物导入、视频导入、游戏导入等。

阅读中(While-reading)

经过阅读前这一阶段的积极思维、猜测、引导，教学步骤很自然地过渡到第二阶段，即阅读时。读中是文本输入，是学生获取信息的初步过程，应采取保持动力、培养技能的教学策略，即在阅读中不断引导学生运用不同的阅读策略进行有效的阅读，掌握各种阅读技能，培养良好的阅读习惯。

1．略读就是选取课文中的重要部分和重要细节，以求抓住主要意思，对课文内容进行总的理解。这一技巧可让学生时刻把注意力集中在课文的主要意思上，学生通过对课文字面意思的理解深入了解整篇课文的含义，并帮助学生深层次地表达自己的见解。

2．扫读通常无须阅读全文，只需找到特定信息所在的段落，然后认真阅读，来了解课文细节。利用这一技巧进行阅读，指导学生寻找课文的有关细节，帮助学生把注意力集中到与主题有关的段落中。这一技巧，使学生能够掌握如何寻找课文细节的正确阅读方式，促进学生对整篇课文进行更深入的理解。

3．泛读也可称为普通阅读，要求学生读懂全文，对全文的主旨大意、主要思想和次要信息及作者的观点有明确的了解。对全文只做一般性的推理、归纳，无须研究细节问题和语法问题。

4．精读要求学生毫无遗漏地仔细阅读全部语言材料并获得对整篇文章深刻而全面的理解，对语篇中的词汇、语法、句式、注释都应仔细领会。

除了以上四种，阅读的微技能还包括：预测，理解大意，猜测词义，推断，理解细节，理解文章结构，理解图表信息，理解指代，理解逻辑关系，理解作者意图，评价阅读内容等。常见的读中活动一般有问答、判断正误、表格、填空、选择题、排序、总结段落大意等。

阅读后(Post-reading)

阅读课的最后阶段，即阅读后阶段，这是检查学生阅读效果的一个重要环节，是引导学生从浅层到深层理解的一个输出过程。读后活动的策略主要是关注理解，促进发展，即帮助学生深层理解课文，理解文章的篇章结构和主旨大意，通过口头、笔头任务实现知识的内化迁移，实现语言技能的综合化，促进综合语言运用能力的提高。教师在这一活动中，应动静相结合，随时获取反馈信息，来检验学生的阅读效果，并随时给学生适合的建议，以便学生在加深对课文理解的基础上，提高他们的实际交际能力。常见的读后活动包含词汇练习、完成段落填空、讨论、辩论、复述、手工、表演、采访、写作、补充阅读等。

总之，阅读课的教学设计要体现"以人为本"的教育理念，要给学生留出阅读的时间和空间，学生能亲自参与阅读的全过程。阅读中通过与文本的互动、学生之间互动、师生之间的互动来获取信息，处理信息，即充分接触语言、理解语言、内化语言、运用语言。

（二）Reading Ⅰ 教学设计案例分析

七上 Unit 2 Let's play sports!

Reading Ⅰ

My favourite football player

Background: Sports

Playing sports is very interesting and good for students' health.

Key words: Sports

Ⅰ Background information

In this lesson, students will go on talking about sports events. They will know about a football player, Li Hua, by reading Simon's article. What's more, students will get some information about football, football players and the World Cup.

Ⅱ Type of the lesson

Reading lesson

Ⅲ Teaching aims and learning objectives

By the end of the lesson, the students will be able to:

1. Memorize the new words and phrases.

2. Guess the meanings of new words and phrases through the pictures or from the context.

3. Form good reading habits and use the reading skills to find the information

in their further study.

4. Experience the feeling of success and team spirit.

5. Learn to be an effective reader and brave to communicate with others in English.

Ⅳ Teaching content

1. New words and expressions

2. Reading skills

Ⅴ Focus of the lesson and predicted area of difficulty

1. New words and expressions

2. How to form and use reading skills

3. How to retell the passage according to the blackboard design

4. How to improve students' involvement in class

Ⅵ Teaching aids

1. Video 2. Pictures 3. Blackboard 4. Chalk

5. Computer 6. Multimedia 7. Projector

Ⅶ Teaching procedures

Step 1 *Warm-up*

Watch a video about different kinds of sports and list names of sports.

【设计理念：观看含有不同体育项目的视频，激发学生对体育的兴趣，同时也唤醒学生本节课学习的热情。视频看完后，鼓励学生尽可能多地说出一些运动项目，既复习了上节课学习的关于体育的单词，也可以根据学生的反应适当教授更多的词汇，寓教于乐，扩大学生的词汇量。师生自由对话谈论自己喜欢的体育运动和运动明星，既活跃了课堂气氛，也调动了学生的课堂积极性。】

T: Boys and girls, before class we watched a short video about sports. There are many sports in it. Can you list them? If you have trouble in saying some, you can say them in Chinese.

football, skating, rowing, cycling, diving, running, fencing, weightlifting, javelin(板书并带读)

T: They are all sport events. Which sport do you like best? Who is your favourite player?

Step 2 *Lead-in*

(1) Present pictures of Messi and ask students some questions to lead in the topic and some new words.

【设计理念：1. 教师通过介绍自己最喜欢的足球运动员梅西，创建了一个真实的语言环境，既调动了学生的积极性，又在和学生的互动中，拉近了与学生的距离。2. 梅西是一名现在很受欢迎的足球明星，被学生们所熟知，这个人物贴近学生的生活。3. 选择呈现梅西的一些精彩的照片，能够吸引学生的注意力，同时在轻松愉悦的课堂氛围下，导入本课的单词和短语，更易于学生接受。4. 对于新词汇的教授也不是生硬刻板的，而是在语境中让学生猜测和理解词义。教师反复带读生词，让学生在课堂上掌握发音和拼写。5. 本环节的设计为下面活动的开展做了铺垫。】

T: Look at the man. Do you know him Messi?

What's he? A football **player**. (板书并带读)

T: Messi is my favourite football player. Do you like him?

How does he look? Yes, he looks strong. (板书并带读)

How does he play football? He plays football **very well**.

So I like him very much!

T: What else do you know about him?

Where is he from?

What football **club** does he play for? Yes, he is a **member** of the football club. (板书并带读 club, member)

Do you know his dream? He wants to play **in the next World Cup**. I hope his **dream** can **come true**. (板书并带读 **in the next World Cup**, **dream**, **come true**)

(2) Show students Simon's picture to lead in the lesson.

【设计理念：介绍完教师自己最爱的足球运动员后，引出 Simon 最喜欢的运动什么，最喜欢的运动员是谁呢。通过几个问题的追问，不仅帮助学生回忆了先前课本中提及的 Simon 的情况，又自然而然过渡到本节课即将学习的内容。】

T: Who is he?

What sport does Simon like?

What does Simon do after school?

T：Do you know who is Simon's favourite football player? Let's turn to Page 20 and read this passage.

Step 3 *Fast reading*

【设计理念：通过自上而下的 skim 阅读方法，理出文章的主线并抓住文章的主旨大意。】

(1) Read quickly and answer the question.

【设计理念：通过快速浏览文章，找出文章主旨大意问题的答案。规范学生的阅读方法，快速默读，对于文章大意题，提醒学生重点阅读文章的标题、开头和末尾。】

Who is Simon's favourite football player?

(2) Read quietly to get the main idea.

【设计理念：浏览文章体会段落大意，梳理段落结构。而给出大意让学生写出相对应的段落，则大大降低了难度。】

Write the correct paragraph numbers according to the main ideas.

Information	Paragraph
What is Li Hua's dream?	________
Who is Li Hua?	________
Who is Simon's favourite football player?	________
What does Li Hua do in his free time?	________

Step 4 *Careful reading*

(1) Read Para. 2 and complete the information.

【设计理念：1. 通过这些阅读活动，训练学生的 scan 阅读能力，使学生获取文章的细节信息并对文章有更深入的理解。2. 教师适时地板书关键词和短语，既帮助学生梳理了文章的脉络，又为后面的语言输出做了铺垫。】

1) Finish the card.

Millie's card about Li Hua	
Name	Li Hua
Age	
Club	
Looks	
Comes from	
Lives in	

T：How old is he?（请一个学生回答并板书22）

Which club is he in?（请一个学生回答并板书 **Huanghe Football Club**）

How does he look?（请一个学生回答并板书 **strong**）

Where does he come from?（请一个学生回答并板书 **Guangdong**）

Where does he live?（请一个学生回答并板书 **Beijing**）

2）Fill in the blanks.

Is Li Hua in any club?

Yes. He's a(n)______ of Huanghe Football Club.

How old is he?

He's ______ years old.

How does he look?

He looks ______ .

Does he come from Beijing?

No, he doesn't. He ______ Guangdong, but now ______ Beijing.

Does he play football well?

Yes, he does. Many people ______ him.

T：Read the dialogue in pairs.

I'll invite two students to read it for us.（请两个学生回答并板书 **a new member of**，**very well**，**like**）

(2) Read Para. 3 and answer questions.

* Does Li Hua play football every day?（请一个学生回答并板书 **play football every day**）

* What does Li Hua do in his free time?（请一个学生回答并板书 **in his free time, study English**）

* What does Li Hua enjoy doing?（请一个学生回答并板书 **enjoy listening to music**）

* Why does Li Hua enjoy music?（请一个学生回答并板书 **make him happy**）

(3) Read Para. 4 and fill in the blanks.

Li Hua wants to ________________.（请一个学生回答并板书 **play in the next World Cup**）

Simon hopes ________________.（请一个学生回答并板书 **come true**）

(4) Read again and do more exercises.

【设计理念：通过抢答的形式来检查学生对文本信息的掌握情况，极大地调动了学生的积极性。】

1) Do true or false questions.

Li Hua is a football player and he is Simon's favourite football star.

Li Hua comes from Beijing, but now lives in Guangdong.

Simon is a new member of Huanghe Football Club.

Li Hua looks strong, but does not play football well.

Li Hua plays football every day, and he studies English in his free time.

Li Hua's dream is to play in the next World Cup.

2) Complete the sentences.

Li Hua is Simon's (1)________ football star.

Li Hua is a(n) (2)________ of Huanghe Football Club.

Li Hua plays football (3)________.

Li Hua (4)________ English in his free time.

Li Hua also (5)________ listening to music. It makes him (6)________.

Li Hua has a(n) (7)________. He wants to play in the (8)________ World Cup.

Step 5 *Post-reading*

【设计理念：1. 运用本节课所学的生词、词组和句型，以采访的形式来复述文章，更加形象生动，符合学生的心理特点，使学生乐于开口说英语。2. 通过创造语言环境，来激活学生对该话题的语言积累，培养学生与他人沟通的能力。】

T：Now boys and girls, please work in pairs. One is a reporter from CCTV, and the other is Simon. Make an interview to talk about Simon's favourite football player, Li Hua, including name, age, football club, be from, live in, looks, hobby, dream, why you like him.

Step 6 *Homework*

【设计理念：1. 巩固课堂所学知识，并能更好地熟悉本篇文章。2. 在小组合作的基础上，开始查阅资料，组织好自己最爱的运动明星的发言稿。3. 本节课学习后，学生能够在现实生活中运用并为以后的学习做准备。】

T：Now please remember your homework：

(1) Remember the new words and phrases.

(2) Retell the article and write it down.

(3) Search for more information about your favourite football player and prepare for your report.

Ⅷ Blackboard design

Unit 2 Reading Ⅰ

My favourite football player—Li Hua

Age：22

Club：a new member of Huanghe Football Club

Comes from：Guangdong

Lives in：Beijing

Looks：strong—very well—like

What he does：play football every day in his free time, study English

enjoy listening to music—make him happy

Wants：play in the next World Cup—come true

Ⅸ Teaching reflection

本课线索清晰，各活动环环相扣，由浅入深，水到渠成，符合学生的认知发展规律。活动设计遵循趣味性、探究性、开放性原则,拓宽了学生的视野,培养了实践能力。

学生对本课的话题很感兴趣,整节课都保持一种互动、轻松、愉快、和谐的学习氛围。

本节课设计了很多活动,学生学习情绪非常高涨,扩大了学生的参与度,提高了积极性。正确处理了教师和学生的角色关系,体现了教师的主导作用和学生的主体地位。在教师的引导和调控下,学生积极配合教师,很好地完成本课的教学目标。

点评:

本节课的教学设计符合新课程标准理念,教学目标明确,教学活动由浅入深,环环相扣。读前活动有三个作用:

1. 观看体育项目的视频激发学生的阅读动机。

2. 呈现足球明星梅西的运动图片为学生激活和提供必要的背景知识,通过简单的问答引出本节课的话题"最喜欢的运动"。

3. 通过看图说话引出新的词汇,为进一步阅读解决理解上的语言障碍。这个步骤是整堂课的一个关键点,是使学生从平和达到兴奋的转折点。用师生都感兴趣的视频和人物,引起师生的共鸣,拉近学生和教师的距离,为创造一个热情的、活跃的、和谐的课堂气氛打下基础。

读中活动的设计重点在培养学生运用略读和扫读两种阅读技巧的能力。略读是眼睛看着阅读材料上的某个预选部分,以获得对所读材料的整体性理解。教师引导学生浏览性阅读全文,回答问题,跳跃式地读,读文章的主旨段、主旨句以获取文章的中心思想和主要内容,进而帮助学生梳理段落结构,了解段落大意。扫读是眼睛为了寻找大脑所需的特定信息而对材料所做的扫视,是寻找特定信息的一种过程。学生通过分段阅读完成信息卡,完成表格、问与答、填空判断正误、完成句子等活动,有目的地查找、获取信息,进行有效阅读,降低了阅读的难度,培养了阅读的技巧,同时使学生体验到学习的乐趣和成功的愉悦。

读后活动设计一个采访的活动来检验阅读的效果,活动形式新颖,能锻炼学生复述课文的能力,让学生进一步熟悉课文内容,巩固所学的语言知识,认识语篇的结构层次和意图层次,体验内含的情感,并学会创造性地运用本课所掌握的语言形式。学生在用中学,学中用,学用结合,体现学以致用的原则，培养学生的语言输出技能。

七下 Unit 6 Outdoor fun

Reading I

Down the rabbit hole

Background: Alice's adventure

Teacher and students follow Alice and get into the Wonderland.

Key words: by a river, on the field, in the hall

I Background information

Alice in Wonderland is a novel written by the English author Lewis Carroll in 1865. It tells a story of a girl named Alice falling through a rabbit hole into a fantasy world populated by peculiar creatures. Students in Grade Seven are familiar with the story and the reading text is adapted from the book. So it is not difficult for them to comprehend the content of the text.

II Type of the lesson

Reading lesson

III Teaching aims and learning objectives

By the end of the lesson, the students will be able to:

1. Understand the meaning of the new words.
   Use them in proper situations.
2. Follow Alice's point of view and share her amazing adventure.
3. Use different reading skills to pinpoint relevant information and key words.
4. Retell what happened to Alice.
5. Cooperate with each other and understand the importance of team work.

IV Teaching content

1. New words
2. The story of *Alice in Wonderland*
3. Different reading skills

V Focus of the lesson and predicted area of difficulty

1. New words and the story of *Alice in Wonderland*
2. Different reading skills

3. How to instruct students to follow Alice's point of view

Ⅵ Teaching aids

1. Blackboard 2. Chalk 3. Computer 4. Multimedia

Ⅶ Teaching procedures

Step 1 *Warm-up and lead-in*

Play a short video about the film *Alice in Wonderland*.

T: What can you see in the video? You can see many strange animals. It is a wonderland. What's the name of the little girl? Yes, her name is Alice. (板书)

Do you know the story? What's the name of the book?

Yes, it's *Alice in Wonderland*. The book is very popular. Have you ever read it? Do you like the book?

Who is the writer? Do you know him? Yes. His name is Lewis Carroll. He wrote the story in 1865. It's really an old story. So which tense is the story in? Yes, it's in the simple past tense.

【设计理念：课前播放一段与本课时密切相关的视频《爱丽丝漫游仙境》的片段。通过视频的播放，调动学生的积极性，吸引学生的注意力，活跃课堂气氛。在导入时，适当地介绍了一些与《爱丽丝漫游仙境》这部作品相关的背景知识，为阅读做准备。】

Step 2 *Down the rabbit hole* (*Fast reading*)

T: Look at the title "Down the rabbit hole". What do you want to know?

Who falls down the rabbit hole?

When does she fall down the rabbit hole?

Where is the rabbit hole?

Why does she fall down the rabbit hole?

How does she fall down the rabbit hole?

What happened to her?

(板书 who, when, where, why, how, what)

Can you find all the answers? Now, you need to read Alice's adventure. OK, please turn your book to Page 78. Read the text quickly and quietly and find out the information you want.

T：How many places are there in the story? How many paragraphs are there in the story? Now match the paragraphs with the places.

（找学生回答）

Now, it's show time. There are **three** places in the story. They are "by the river", "on the filed", and "in the hall"（板书）. There are five paragraphs. **Paras. 1 – 2** happened by the river. **Para. 3** happened on the field. **Paras. 4 – 5** happened in the hall.（板书）

【设计理念：让学生根据标题，发挥自己的想象力，推测故事情节的发展也是训练学生阅读能力的一种方式。所以，在快速阅读之前，先让学生根据标题推测故事主要内容。有了思考和预设之后，再让学生通过泛读理清文本结构，从而促进学生对文本的理解。】

Step 3 *Alice's adventure* (*Careful reading*)

(1) What happened by the river?（Paras. 1–2）

T：What happened in the first place "by the river"? Please read Paras. 1–2 carefully and find who was by the river and what they did.

（学生分小组讨论，找到相关人物，并在文中找到动词）

T：Are you ready? Let me check your answers.（核对答案）

Alice	The rabbit
sat by a river	passed by
looked up	said
heard a sound	took a watch
saw a rabbit	looked at the time

T：Alice saw a rabbit. What did Alice think of the rabbit? Why did Alice think it was amazing?

（找一个学生回答）

T：Yes. The rabbit was amazing. It was in a coat. It took a watch out of its pocket and looked at the time. And it could speak. It said, "Oh, dear! I'll be late!"（板书）

【设计理念：快速阅读之后，学生还需要进一步细读文本，了解文章的具体内容。第一个阅读任务就是精读第一、二段，找到关键人物以及他们做了

什么。这个环节可以让学生更有效地梳理故事情节的发展。】

（2）What happened on the field?（Para. 3）

T：What happened in the second place "on the field"? What did Alice do after seeing the amazing rabbit? Please read Para. 3 and find the answers.

T：Did you find the answers? Hands up! At first, Alice stood up, ran across the field after the rabbit and then jumped down the rabbit hole(板书).

T：Please think, if you see such a rabbit, how will you feel? What will you do? Run after it or not? Why?（打开学生思维）

【设计理念：先让学生精读第三段，找出 Alice 在看到兔子之后做了什么。然后再让学生发挥创造力，设身处地思考"如果是自己遇到了兔子，会有怎样的感受和做法？"这个 further thinking 在阅读课型中的运用，可以给课堂带来更多的生成，让学生的思维能力得到提升。】

（3）What happened in the hall?（Paras. 4–5）

T：So Alice jumped down the rabbit hole. Then what happened?

Read the following text and guess the meaning of the words with the context clues.（阅读技巧一：根据上下文猜词义）

Down, down, down. Alice fell for a long time, and then she **hit** the ground.

She found **herself alone** in a long, **low** hall.

T：What's the meaning of the word?（带读）. If I change the passage into this：

Alice fell for a long time, and then she **got to** the ground. She found **she was** in a **small** hall.

T：Compare the two passages.（阅读技巧二：体会用词的精准性）Which one is better? Why? So the three "down"s imply Alice fell for a long time. The verb "hit" emphasizes that there is a crash when she got to the ground. And "herself" and "alone" emphasize that Alice is some kind of helpless. The two words "long" and "low" make the description more vivid.

T：What could Alice see in the hall? What kind of problems did she have?（学生小组讨论并展示）

T：Alice could see doors all around, but they were all locked. She could see a key on the table, but it did not fit any of the doors. She wanted to go through the door, but she was too big.

【设计理念：根据上下文猜测词义的能力，在阅读理解中起着非常重要的作用。在让学生精读第四、五段，完成阅读任务之前，挑出较难的段落，让学生猜测生词含义，可以训练学生对上下文信息的捕捉和联想能力，体会用词精准的重要性。】

(4) Retell the story

T：Now can you find the answers to the questions?

Who? When? Where? Why? What? How?

(Show students pictures and retell the story)

T：Now, boys and girls, do you still remember what happened to Alice? Please put the following sentences in the correct order.

T：Are you ready? Let's check your answers.

【设计理念：复述课文是为了引导学生回顾整个故事的情节发展，从而巩固学生对文本的理解，加深对文章内容的印象。】

(5) Simon's notes

T：So everyone, do you like the story? Our friend Simon makes some notes about the story. But there are some mistakes in his notes. Now you need to help him check his notes about the story. Write a "T" or "F". If it is false, try to correct it.

T：Now Simon is asking Sandy some questions about the story. This time you need to complete their dialogue.

【设计理念：通过处理课本上的练习，进一步巩固学生对文本内容的记忆和理解。】

Step 4 *Post-reading*

T：You know Alice couldn't go through the door because she was too large. How can she go through the door? What will she do then? Do you have some interesting and amazing ideas? Now think about it.

T：What do you think of Alice? Do you like her? Is she careful, clever, curious, friendly, brave? Why do you think so?

T：Today we had a great time together with Alice. Are you happy? Me too. I think Alice is a curious and brave girl. With curiosity and bravery, we can see a totally different world. Do you want to know what really happened next? Maybe you can find the book and read more. Reading is fun.

【设计理念：读后活动让学生发散思维，激发想象，并对 Alice 这一人物性格进行探讨和评价，是对文本内容的升华。】

Step 5 *Homework*

T: Now please remember your homework.

(1) Retell the story by yourself and share with each other.

(2) Find out what happened next and enjoy reading the novel *Alice in Wonderland* in your free time.

【设计理念：通过课后复述课文内容，巩固课堂所学的语言信息。对这部作品感兴趣的同学，还可以进行更多的课外阅读。】

Ⅷ Blackboard design

7B Unit 6 Outdoor fun—Reading Ⅰ

Down the rabbit hole

who, when, where, why, what, how

By a river

Alice	The rabbit
sat by a river	passed by
looked up	said
heard a sound	took a watch
saw a rabbit	looked at the time

On the field

ran across the field

jumped down the hole

stood up

In the hall

doors all around	They were all locked.
a key on the table	It didn't fit any of the doors.
through the door	She was too big.

Ⅸ Teaching reflection

本节课主要任务是阅读 Reading 部分的课文，训练学生使用阅读技能解决问题的能力。课堂的各个环节设计合理、结构完整、过渡自然、不乏新意，学生的参与度较高，积极性也被很好地调动了起来，课堂效果较好。

课文的内容是《爱丽丝梦游仙境》的片段。为了增强学生的兴趣，减轻阅读障碍，在课前播放了影片《爱丽丝漫游仙境》的一个片段。通过视频的播放，学生的积极性明显被调动了起来，注意力也相当集中。在影片结束后，又对其中的人物、作者和时态做了介绍，让学生了解与这部作品相关的背景知识，为之后的阅读奠定基石。

阅读环节的设计非常丰富，由读前预设、快速阅读、精细阅读、读后活动等板块组成。每一个阅读任务都有十分明确的目的性，而且题目类型的设计也是别具一格，学生在一个接一个的任务中，仍然感到兴趣盎然，一点儿也不乏味。

课后作业的设计也与阅读这一主题紧紧相扣，为喜欢阅读的孩子提供了更多提升阅读能力的机会。

本节课的特色就是不单单依靠做题来串联整个阅读过程，让学生发挥自己的想象力和创造力，推测故事情节的发展也是一种较为创新的方式。因为有了思考和预设，学生对文本内容的渴望被点燃，阅读的兴趣也大大增加了。

但是这节课也存在一些不足和需要改进的地方。在生词和新短语的教授上，还要再细化。老师要增加带读的次数，还要在适当的情境中，对重点词汇和短语进行操练，让学生真正地理解所学的新知识。

点评：

本节课设计的读前活动利用文章标题“Down the rabbit hole”，提出六个问题，预测文章的内容是一个亮点。充分利用标题可以预测阅读材料的大意，降低阅读的难度，学生在阅读过程中验证自己的预测，调动参与阅读的积极性，激发阅读欲望；利用标题生成问题菜单，提升学生分析文本的能力。我们在教学实践中还可以利用标题凸显关键段落，化解学习的难点；利用标题深度解读文本，对课文进行深度理解和升华阅读，以培养学生的思维能力和阅读技能。

精读课文占据读中活动的主体，教师将阅读分为三层，即字面阅读、推理阅读和形象阅读。在字面意义理解的基础上，指导学生根据文本的细节材料对深层含义做出推理、推论，激发学生的思维力和想象力。教师把更多的时间交给学生，将学生的各个感觉器官调动起来，去寻找文章中的两个关键人物以及他们的活动；运用 further thinking 提升学生的思维能力；组织学生猜测词义，体会用词的精准，引导学生仔细地阅读课文，理解课文，去寻找问题并且解决问题，构建起初步的全文语义图像。

读后活动设计开放性的问题，基于学生已经掌握的知识，要求学生充分发挥想象，就 Alice 的故事如何进一步发展，以及 Alice 这个人物性格特征进行讨论，进一步拓展学生的视野，使学生产生浓厚的学习兴趣，以激发学生的思考和求知欲，训练和培养学生的思维能力，促使学生在不断的思考和探索中发展创造力。

整个教学环节的设计始终坚持：设问→思考→交流→创造→升华；教师活动的设计始终坚持：质疑→引问→启迪→激励→提炼→拓伸；学生活动的设计始终坚持：发现问题→提出方案→交流论证→实践创造→总结领悟。

作业的布置也值得一提。教师布置学生进一步进行课后延伸阅读，以课内带课外，以精读带博读，不断开拓学生的视野，丰富学生的语言积累。

八上 Unit 4 Do it yourself

Reading I

My cousin and DIY

Background: My DIY jobs

Key words: DIY jobs

Ⅰ Background information

In this unit, students learn mainly about DIY. DIY stands for "do it yourself". Students can know some funny things about DIY according to Suzy's story. Suzy's cousin Andrew is crazy about DIY but he is not good at it.

Ⅱ Type of the lesson

Reading lesson

Ⅲ Teaching aims and learning objectives

By the end of the lesson, the students will be able to:

1. Understand the meanings of the new words and use them in proper situations.
2. Understand the passage and finish the exercises.
3. Describe a DIY activity with some new words.
4. Show great interest in DIY.
5. Analyze the phrases and sentences to get a better understanding.
6. Get more detailed information about Andrew and his DIY jobs.

Ⅳ Teaching content

1. New words
2. Different reading skills

Ⅴ Focus of the lesson and predicted area of difficulty

1. New words

2. How to have a better understanding of the passage

3. Different reading skills

Ⅵ Teaching aids

1. Blackboard

2. Multimedia

Ⅶ Teaching procedures

Step 1 (*Warm-up and lead-in*)

(1) Free talk

【设计理念：通过一些简单的对话，让学生熟悉英语的语言环境，引起学生对 DIY 的学习兴趣，用师生对话活跃课堂气氛，调动学生的学习积极性。】

T: What do you often do in your free time?

Guess what I often do in my free time.

Do you know DIY?

Do you like DIY? Give us some examples.

Do you want to know my DIY stories?

(2) Show my DIY story

【设计理念：通过老师的 DIY 故事，了解制作丝网花的过程，把一些重要的短语导出来，让学生在听故事的同时可以了解生词，扫清阅读的障碍。】

T: Look at this. (展示一个手工发卡) What's this? A hair clip. Is it beautiful? It's special for me.

Because I made it instead of buying it.

I am crazy about DIY. I am also crazy about making stockings flowers. But at first, I was not very good at making them. So once I made a mistake. I wanted to make a rose. But it looked terrible.

Did it look like a rose?

It didn't look like a rose. Instead, it looked like a lily. It looked like a lily instead of a rose.

What should I do? My sister advised me to take a course in making flowers.

So I attended the lessons and the teacher asked me to buy some books. And I put up a shelf. Put those books on the shelf.

After attending the lessons, I got better at making stockings flowers. Now not only my sister but also I like making stockings flowers.

Step 2 *Reading*

(1) Pre-reading

【设计理念：在读文章之前让学生对文章有一个大概的预测，提高之后阅读的准确性。】

T: Do you want to know more about DIY? Suzy's cousin Andrew is also crazy about DIY. Is he good at DIY?

(2) While-reading

【设计理念：通过不同形式的练习让学生对文章有更加深入的了解，形式单一的阅读题目会让学生觉得枯燥和乏味，失去对阅读的兴趣，所以不同的题型有助于激发学生的阅读兴趣。】

① T: Can you find out the main idea of each paragraph?

- Para. 1 Introduction of Andrew
- Paras. 2 – 4 Andrew's DIY jobs
- Para. 5 Advice from Suzy

② Read Para. 1 and answer questions.

- a. What does he love doing?
- b. How is the house when he finishes?

③ Read Paras. 2 – 4 and find out problems Andrew caused.

a. Putting in a brighter light—The whole house had a power cut.

b. Putting up a picture—He hit a pipe and filled the room with water.

c. Painting the living room blue—Now the living room has not only blue walls but also a blue ceiling and floor.

d. Putting up a shelf—No books could stay on the shelf because one end of the shelf was much higher than the other.

④ Pair work

Suzy: I want a shelf ... bed.

Andrew: No ...

(half a day later)

Suzy: Wow, how long did you do it?

Andrew: I spent … putting up the shelf. Isn't it great?

Suzy: Whoops. The books cannot stay there because ... of the shelf is ... than ...

⑤ Further thinking

【设计理念:启发学生的想象力和思维,让学生更加积极地参与课堂。】

T: We know one end of the shelf was much higher than the other.

Think about the ways to solve the problem.

⑥ Match the jobs with the problems. (B2)

putting in a brighter light	c. The whole house had a power cut.
putting up a picture	b. He hit a pipe and filled the room with water.
painting the living room	d. The cat is blue now.
putting up a shelf	a. No books could stay on it.

⑦ Read Para. 5 Advice from Suzy

Suzy ________ some books about DIY for Andrew and also ________ him to take a course in DIY. But this made him ________ because he says he knows ________ about it. So ________, Suzy is reading all the books herself and ________ lessons every Saturday. Now she knows ________ more about DIY than Andrew.

⑧ Further thinking

【设计理念:增加阅读文章的趣味性,同时也增加文章阅读的深度和广度,让学生不仅仅思考文本,而且拓展学生的思维,为想象力插上翅膀。】

a. What should we do when we do DIY jobs?

b. What do you think of Andrew?

Be crazy about DIY

Never give up DIY

Not really good at DIY

Stubborn

⑨ Read and do T/F questions (B3)

Suzy's cousin loves doing DIY.

Suzy's cousin failed to put in a new light in his bedroom.

Suzy's cousin put a picture on a pipe.

Suzy's cousin thought the cat was boring, so he painted it blue.

It took Suzy's cousin only a few minutes to put up the shelf on the wall.

Suzy's cousin wants to get better at DIY.

⑩ Complete the conversation

Suzy: My cousin Andrew is (1) ____________ about DIY. He loves to (2) ____________ things and decorate his house.

Kitty: What kind of things does he do?

Suzy: He once tried to put in a brighter light in his bedroom, but he made a (3) ____________, and his house had a (4) ____________.

Kitty: Oh dear!

Suzy: And last month, he thought the living room was (5) ____________, so he painted the walls (6) ____________. But he also painted the ceiling, the floor and even the cat!

Kitty: Oh no!

Suzy: He once spent five hours putting up a (7) ____________ on the wall for me, but my books couldn't stay there because one end of the shelf was much (8) ____________ than the other.

Kitty: He should take a(n) (9) ____________ in DIY.

Suzy: But he says he already knows (10) ____________ about it!

(3) Post-reading

【设计理念：通过一些活动让学生对文章有更加深入的了解，复述故事可以提高学生的思维连贯性和语篇意识。】

Retell the story

Step 3 *Group work*

Making a love envelope

【设计理念：让学生通过本节课的学习掌握关于 DIY 制作的英文表达方法，从而尝试写出自己的 DIY 故事。这个活动旨在帮助学生练习巩固本节课所学的 DIY 制作的英文表达方法。】

T: Do you know why I love DIY so much? I am crazy about it not only because it is interesting but also because it can help others. We know many people in the world need our help. We can make a love envelope to help them. Do you want to help them?

Are you ready to make it?

Do you know how to make it?

1. Prepare a piece of heart-shaped paper.

2. Draw some pictures or write some sentences on it.

3. Remember to fold not only the two sides but also the bottom side.

Step 4 *Homework*

【设计理念：1. 巩固课堂所学的重要的知识点。2. 学会用英语描述自己的 DIY 故事。3. 对有关英语的 DIY 学习产生浓厚的兴趣。】

(1) Recite the text.

(2) Finish the exercises.

(3) Try to write something about your own DIY stories.

Ⅷ Blackboard design

8A Unit 4 Do it yourself—Reading Ⅰ

My cousin and DIY

New words

- Para. 1 Introduction of Andrew
- Paras. 2 – 4 Andrew's DIY jobs
- Para. 5 Advice from Suzy

Ⅸ Teaching reflection

本节课的教学目标是学会 DIY 的相关词汇，读懂并能理解文章的内容并完成相关练习，引导学生的 DIY 意识。

这是一堂英语阅读课。如何激发学生的阅读兴趣，在有限的时间里可以读懂文章，并掌握一些阅读技巧和方法，养成良好的阅读习惯，这是我在准备这节课之前一直考虑的问题。

我知道阅读的兴趣和能力的培养不是一蹴而就的，这需要老师精心设计课堂，以科学有效的方法来引导学生阅读，并且在阅读的过程中同时提高学生的听说读写能力。为了达成这些目标，我在这节课中进行了以下几个方面的尝试：

一、故事性的生词导入

Reading 课型不可避免地会有很多生词，这是学生阅读中的拦路虎，为了消灭这些拦路虎,第一部分要在情景中导入生词,本单元是以 DIY 为主的,所以我选择的方式是用自己 DIY 故事来导入生词。通过自己制作丝网花的过程,让学生在听故事的过程中理解生词的意义。

二、多样的阅读题型训练

My cousin and DIY 这篇阅读文章一共有 5 段,分为三个部分: Introduction of Andrew, Andrew's DIY jobs, Advice from Suzy。每一个部分分别设置不同的题型,比如介绍部分比较简单,可以设置比较容易的问答题。main body 部分用图片的形式让学生加深对阅读内容以及细节的理解。最后一个部分设置成任务型阅读的题型,让学生对文章有更深层次的认识。

当学生有了阅读兴趣之后,有效的阅读技巧就显得尤为重要了。本节课存在的问题是对于阅读技巧的训练不充分,缺乏对学生阅读策略的指导,使得一部分学生在阅读过程中无从下手,不知道怎么捕捉有效的消息,阻碍了学生做出正确的推理和判断。

点评:

本节课的教学设计将培养学生的阅读兴趣和养成良好的阅读习惯放在了首要的地位。在导入新课时,教师和学生分享了自己的 DIY 的故事,并且展示自己的 DIY 作品,吸引学生的眼球,激起学生的阅读欲望。美国教育家哈曼说过:“那些不设法勾起学生求知欲望的教学,正如同捶打着一块冰冷的生铁。”一篇文章如果导入的精彩,就犹如给这篇文章披上一层神秘的面纱,使得学生跃跃欲试想一睹文章的芳容。课堂活动能吸引学生,那么学生就更愿意付出努力去阅读。接着教师鼓励学生大胆地猜测文章的内容,设计富有挑战性的阅读任务: 找出段落大意、问与答、发现问题、两两对话、深层思考、匹配、提建议、讨论 Andy 这个人物的特点、补全对话等;教师引导学生在限定的时间内有任务地阅读、思考或讨论,得出完成任务的构思和方案,坚持让学生充分运用语言来解决一系列的问题,使学生感受到英语的魅力,激发学生的阅读兴趣。特别值得一提的是 further-thinking、提建议和讨论人物的特点这些活动,教师对语言内容和情景进行适当的改编,使这些环节的活动更加生动、自然,富有感染力,激发学生的想象力,提升语言输出的质量。爱因斯坦曾说过,想象力比知识更重要,因为知识是有限的,而想象力概括着世界上的一切,是知识进化的源泉。

读后活动要求学生以小组为单位制作爱心信封,体现了教师重视对学生情感态度与价值观的培养。学生在动眼、动口、动脑、动手中进行小组合作，培养学生的合作精神。积极调动不同层次学生参与小组活动，展示特长，发挥作用，团结协作，激发持续的学习热情，不断使学生体验成功，实现学生的自我价值。

八下　Unit 7　International charities

Reading Ⅰ

An interview with an ORBIS doctor

Background: International charities

Everyone should try his best to help different kinds of international charities to help those who need help around us because we are family.

Keywords: International charities, ORBIS, blindness, Flying Eye Hospital, Dr. Ma

Ⅰ　Background information

ORBIS helps blind people in poor countries. The state of being blind is called blindness. Why does ORBIS help the blind patients? Because blindness affects many people around the world, mostly in poor countries. But most of the cases of blindness can be prevented or cured. Why don't the blind go to see doctors? Because they are so poor that they can't pay for medical treatment. ORBIS doctors treat them for free. They operate on/do (perform) operations on their patients. So the patients are thankful/grateful to them. How do you think ORBIS doctors feel when they help people? (Of course, they feel very proud.) Everyone should try his best to help different kinds of international charities to help those who need help around us because we are family.

Ⅱ　Type of the lesson

Reading lesson

Ⅲ　Teaching aims

By the end of the lesson, students should be able to:

1. Memorize the new words and phrases.

2. Guess the meanings of new words and phrases through the pictures or from the context.

3. Form good reading habits and use the reading skills to find the information in their further study.

4. Experience the feeling of success and team spirit.

5. Learn to be an effective reader and brave to communicate with others in English.

Ⅳ Teaching content

1. New words and phrases

2. Reading skills

3. Learn to help people

Ⅴ Focus of the lesson and predicted area of difficulty

1. New words and phrases

2. Retelling

3. Reading skills

Ⅵ Teaching aids

1. Pictures 2. Blackboard 3. Chalk 4. Computer

5. Multimedia 6. Projector

Ⅶ Teaching procedures

Step 1 *Pre-reading(about 7 – 8 mins.)*

【设计理念：首先教师通过回顾上一课时 Welcome 课型中所学的几个慈善组织，积极帮助学生创设一个真实而又轻松的语言学习环境，充分调动学生的学习积极性，激发他们阅读英语的兴趣。更重要的是为他们正式的英语阅读提供和主题相关的背景知识，同时培养他们的语篇赏析能力。教师在精心设计的情境下，自然地导入英语生词，为课堂上其他相关的语言活动做好必要的铺垫。】

T：Yesterday we learnt something about international charities. What international charities do you know?

S：ORBIS

Oxfam

UNICEF

WWF

T：Who does it help?

S: …

T: How does it help?

S:	ORBIS	the blind in poor areas uses its Flying Eye Hospital
	Oxfam	poor people
	UNICEF	build a better world for … ,especially …
		provide basic education for …
		work for the equal rights of …
		work to prevent the spread of …
	WWF	environment & wild animals

(板书: Blind Flying Eye Hospital)

Step 2 *While-reading (about 19 – 22 mins.)*

(1) Fast reading(about 3 – 5 mins.)

【设计理念:运用自上而下模式,让学生在任务型教学模式的指导下熟练运用合适的阅读策略进行快速阅读。】

Activity 1　Free talk

T: Amy is interested in ORBIS. She found an interview with an ORBIS doctor. Who is the doctor?

S: Dr. Ma.

T: I put this interview into four parts.

Lines 1 – 6, 7 – 15, 16 – 20, 21 – 26.

Activity 2　Tell the main idea

【设计理念:让学生在任务型教学模式的指导下熟练运用扫读策略进行快速阅读。】

T: Read and find the main ideas of each paragraph.

S:	Lines 1 – 6	sth. about blindness
	Lines 7 – 15	the work of ORBIS
	Lines 16 – 20	Dr. Ma's work and his feeling
	Lines 21 – 26	Dr. Ma's hope

(2) Careful reading(about 16 – 17 mins.)

【设计理念:精读训练旨在让学生通过多个不同任务的达成培养和运用相关的阅读技巧,从而使学生在教师的指导下进一步加深对文章的理解,体

会文本细节处理的艺术。】

Activity 1 Fill in the blanks

T：First, read Part 1 Something about blindness and fill in the blanks.

S：Blindness	About 285 million people around the world are blind, or have eyes problems, mostly in poor areas.
Something good	About 80 percent of these cases can be prevented or cured.
Something bad	Many people don't have money for medical treatment.

Activity 2 Retell

【设计理念：让学生在任务型教学模式的指导下熟练运用思维导图或关键词句进行文本输出的复述操练。】

S：(Retell)

Activity 3 Answer the questions

【设计理念：让学生在任务型教学模式的指导下掌握任务型阅读答题技巧,以及根据文本进行寻读的能力。】

T：So ORBIS helps them. Then how does ORBIS help? Read Part 2 (Lines 7 – 15) and answer.

S：ORBIS uses its Flying Eye Hospital to visit poor areas.

T：There volunteer doctors ____________.

S：Do operations.

T：Where do they do operations?

S：On the plane.

T：So the plane is also used as ____________.

S：A training plane

Activity 4 Retell

【设计理念：让学生在任务型教学模式的指导下熟练运用思维导图或关键词句进行文本输出的复述操练。】

T：Now let's retell together.

S：...

T：Why don't they work in a hospital?

S：Patients.

Many of our patients can't afford to go to hospital, so we have to go to them.

Local doctors and nurses.

They are invited on board.

T：What can local doctors and nurses do on the plane?

Learn about ___________.

Learn about ___________.

S：Eye operations, new skills

T：They hope to help more people by ___________.

S：Training them

Activity 5　Make a flow chart

【设计理念：流程图的设计旨在帮助学生进一步把握文本篇章的结构和功能。大多数学生在细节处理方面可能比较好，但总结概括的能力一般都比较弱，所以非常有必要平时对学生进行这方面的操练】

T：Read again Lines 7－15 and make a flow chart to show how ORBIS helps people.

S：ORBIS, a charity

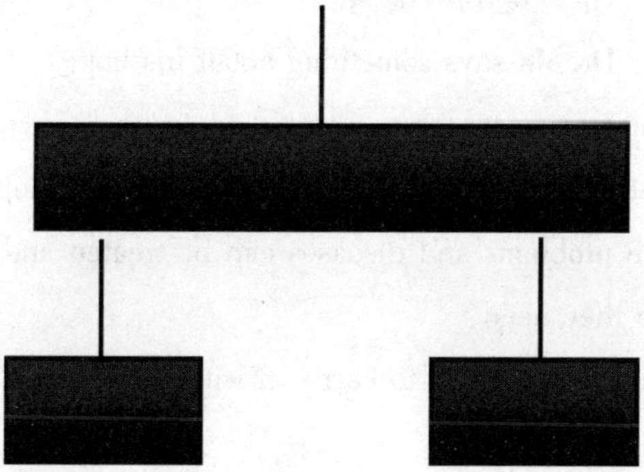

…

Activity 6　Retell

【设计理念：让学生在任务型教学模式的指导下熟练运用思维导图或关键词句进行文本输出的复述操练。】

T：Now try to retell them.

S：…

Activity 7　Answer the questions

【设计理念：让学生在任务型教学模式的指导下掌握任务型阅读答题技巧，以及根据文本进行寻读的能力。】

T：We know Dr. Ma is a volunteer doctor there. Now read Part 3 Lines 16 – 20 and answer how many operations Dr. Ma does during a visit.

S：During the last visit, 150 patients were operated on.

T：The interviewer and Dr. Ma have different feelings.

S：The interviewer says, "You're doing a really important job."

Dr. Ma says, "I'm proud to help people see again and improve their lives."

Activity 8　Retell

【设计理念：让学生在任务型教学模式的指导下熟练运用思维导图或关键词句进行文本输出的复述操练。】

T：Please retell Part 3 according to the chart.

S：…

Activity 9　Read and answer & Retell

【设计理念：让学生在任务型教学模式的指导下掌握任务型阅读答题技巧，以及根据文本进行寻读的能力。同时教师特别注重在学生语言学习的输入和输出方面进行一定程度的平衡。】

T：In last part, Dr. Ma says something about his hope.

Read and answer：

① What can happen when modern medicine is developing quickly?

More eye problems and diseases can be treated and cured.

② What do they need?

More money is needed to carry on with their work.

S：…

T：More people will support them. Now let's retell this part.

S：…

Step 3 *Post-reading: Group work (about 8 – 10 mins.)*

【设计理念：这个小组活动旨在让学生在适合的语言环境中，主动参与到和主题相关的交流与讨论中，从而帮助学生加深对 ORBIS 的理解。】

T：Now suppose some of your group members work in ORBIS. They are volunteer doctors. The other students have eye problems and want to get help from ORBIS. Now make up a dialogue, and ask for the information you want to know about ORBIS. 3 minutes to prepare.

S: …

Step 4 *Homework*

【设计理念：作业设计旨在让学生温故知新。古语曰：凡事预则立，不预则废。预习新知也是学习必不可少的一个环节。】

(1) Recite the whole passage.

(2) Preview Reading 2.

Ⅷ Blackboard design

8B Unit 7 International charities—Reading Ⅰ

An interview with an ORBIS doctor

Blindness 285 million → blind / → eye problems mostly

80% cases can be prevented or cured

don't have money for medical treatment

Work can't afford to … , so … → eye operations

also, … are invited on board → new skills ⇨

by training them

Dr. Ma's work 150 were operated on

feelings → important / → be proud to do

Hope modern medicine ⇨ be treated and cured

is developing quickly

is needed

carry on with

Ⅸ Teaching reflection

本节课能很好地帮助学生在进行不同阅读策略的训练的同时加深对文本的理解力和解读力。学生在教师的精心指导下能够一步一个脚印，有条不紊地进行泛读和精读。

这节课优点在于：首先，课堂一开始从复习上一课型 Welcome 的 4 个慈善组织入手，学生很轻松且拥有较好的情感进入到英语课堂中来。其次，教师将部分新学的生词短语放到具体的情境中去呈现和学习，而不是单纯地灌输单调的词性变化。最后，老师所设计的活动贴近学生生活和学生的当前认知水平，学生易于理解和接受。

但是老师没有把控好课堂活动的时间，导致最后一个活动学生展现的人数不是很多。

点评：

整节课的设计运用“自上而下”的教学模式，以任务型教学方式展开。这种模式是通过师生互动、生生互动中从课堂预设到动态形成。教师从“学”的角度来设计教学内容，学生的活动具有明确的目标及指向具体的操作要求。

读前活动设计了一个 3—4 分钟的复习环节，教师采用谈话的方式和学生进一步熟悉一些慈善机构，共同探讨有关慈善机构的背景知识，通过不断丰富背景知识来刺激学生通过联想自己的既存知识来挖掘即将学习的相关知识，突出背景知识对理解的作用。

读中活动中设计了自由对话、找到段落的主旨大意、填空、回答问题、制作流程图以及复述课文等活动。在每一项的活动中，学生的大脑始终处于一种激活状态，引起学生的共鸣和兴趣，所以整个学习过程都是积极主动的，学生有话可说，有感而发，他们获得的不仅仅是现成的知识点，还有语言运用的能力。而且随着教学任务的不断深化以及学生语言能力的不断提高，整个语言学习的过程会越趋自动化和自主化，学生越能创造性地表达自己的思想。并且在每一个教学环节中教师都有一些微技能的渗透，且不停地提示学生阅读技巧。教师在整个过程中始终是语言习得的促进者、答疑者和向导。师生的语言活动是语言感知→语言理解→操练交际→运用创新，最后实现融会贯通。

本设计在复述课文环节辅助思维导图，就像拿着地图走路一样，学生在记忆所学的阅读材料时不再逐字逐句地“背”英语，而是依据一定的线索“说”

英语，培养学生辨认中心思想、记忆具体事实和重要细节的习惯，实现框架到成文的质变。思维导图的运用能发散学生的思维，有效地激发、丰富和巩固阅读过程中所需的语言图式、内容图式和形式图式。作者可以尝试在读前阶段，利用思维导图激活学生的背景知识和已有的语言知识；在读中阶段，运用思维导图丰富学生的语言知识、篇章结构和内容话题；在读后阶段，通过思维导图巩固学生的内容、语言和形式图式，运用思维导图帮助学生提高对阅读材料的深层理解和评价性理解的能力，记忆阅读材料和运用阅读材料的信息进行交流的能力。

九上　Unit 2　Colours

Reading Ⅰ

The power of colours

Background: There is a relationship between colours and moods.

Teachers help students find out the relationship between colours and moods by reading an article.

Key words: colours, moods

Ⅰ　Background information

Some surveys say that there is a relationship between colours and moods. Each colour may represent some special moods. As a result, people can change their moods by choosing different colours to wear. Students in Grade 9 want to find out what the different colours represent and how they influence us.

Ⅱ　Type of the lesson

Reading lesson

Ⅲ　Teaching aims and learning objectives

By the end of the lesson, the students will be able to:

1. Understand the meanings of the new words and use them in proper situations.

2. Know about different types of colours and what they represent.

3. Develop their reading skills including fast reading and skimming and scanning.

4. Talk about their own favourite colours and see if they match their own

characteristics.

5. Cooperate with partners and use proper colours to change moods.

Ⅳ Teaching content

1. New words and expressions

2. Different colours and what they represent

3. Different reading skills

Ⅴ Focus of the lesson and predicted area of difficulty

1. New words and expressions

2. Different reading skills

3. How to lead students to talk about their own favourite colours and characteristics

Ⅵ Teaching aids

1. Blackboard 2. Chalk 3. Computer 4. Multimedia

5. Projector

Ⅶ Teaching procedures

Step 1 *Free talk and lead-in*

(1) Play a video about colours to lead in the topic of colours.

【设计理念：本课话题是颜色的力量，要讲的是颜色能够影响人的情绪，所以课前播放关于颜色的视频，能迅速激起学生对于颜色的兴趣，引入话题。】

T：Boys and girls, just now we watched a video.

Do you know what it is about? How many colours can you see?

T：Yes! It's about different colours. What are they? Which is your favourite one?

(2) Show several pictures and introduce the types of colours and what they represent.

【设计理念：由颜色视频导入到各种颜色所代表的含义和用法。会拼、会读与颜色相关的单词，会运用重点句式。在教学过程中，注重单词的拼写和音标教学以及四会单词的带读和拼读以及重点句式的操练。】

T：OK. Different people like different colours. Actually, different colours have different meanings and are used in different situations.

Step 2 *Fast reading*

Ask students to read the article quickly.

【设计理念：学生通过快速阅读文章找到两个问题的答案。通过此步骤学生可以对文章有个大致了解，并且能够锻炼学生的快速阅读能力。】

T：Read the passage about colours and what they represent quickly and find out the answers to the two questions.

T：Read quickly and answer the two questions：

① How many kinds of colours are talked about in the text?

② What are they?

Step 3 *Careful reading*

Read the passage paragraph by paragraph and try to finish these tasks. Read more carefully.

（1）Read Para. 1 and answer the true or false questions.

（2）Read Para. 2 and try to fill in the blanks about calm colours.

（3）Read Para. 3 about warm colours and answer the three questions.

（4）Read Para. 4 about energetic colours and answer the three questions.

（5）Read Para. 5 about strong colours and try to complete the passage.

【设计理念：在快速阅读已经对文章有所了解的基础上进行更加细致的细读，能够帮助学生更好地锻炼阅读能力。第一段设置的是判断正误，第二段是填空，第三、四段是回答问题，第五段是完成短文。每一段设置不同形式的任务，帮助学生锻炼不同的阅读能力，也有益于防止学生因觉得枯燥而失去阅读兴趣。】

Step 4 *Post-reading & Practice*

Read the passage again and try to finish the exercises.

【设计理念：在全文阅读完成后，用书后练习帮助学生用不同形式的任务对全文再次进行回顾。】

T：Now you have learned a lot about colours and their meanings.

① What do colours represent?

② Finish a summary.

③ Finish the questionnaire with your own information.

Pair work (Talk about their questionnaire)

【设计理念：让学生根据问卷两两合作完成对话。在完成对话时，注重语音和语调的培养和指正，提高学生的口语水平。及时给有困难的学生提供帮助。】

T：Just now you have finished the questionnaire about your own favourite colour. Please work with your partner and interview each other about your favourite colour.

Step 5 *Group work*

【设计理念：在具体的情境中进行当堂反馈，让学生先在组内讨论再进行对话，能够扩大学生的参与面。内容贴近学生生活，能够帮助学生将所学知识灵活运用到实际生活中。】

T：This is Tom. He will take part in a football match this week. This is Lucy. She will have an exam tomorrow, so she feels sad. What should they wear? What colours should they choose? Discuss with your group members and try to give them some suggestions.

Step 6 *Homework*

【设计理念：学生完成课后作业并与家人朋友一起讨论本课所学。通过这样的作业争取让每一个孩子将当堂所学知识加以应用。】

T：You really have done a great job. Here is your homework：

① Read the passage.

② Finish exercises.

③ Give suggestions to your friends and families about what colours they should wear.

Ⅷ Blackboard design

Unit 2 Colours

Reading Ⅰ

wisdom	strong→strength	prefer sth.
pure→purity		green with envy
create	grow→growth	on one's wedding day
envy	heat	require

Ⅸ Teaching reflection

本课在设计时突出体现了 Reading 课型增加学生生词量和训练学生阅读技巧的教学目标。在导入时与本课主题相联系,以视频的方式导入,使得学生注意力被充分吸引到课堂上来。在导入过程中,同样引入了多种形式的呈现方式,大量的图片信息可以防止学生在听课时疲劳走神。教学内容按照由词到句、由句到篇的方式安排,层层递进,充分考虑学生的学习规律,帮助学生掌握新知。在新知识导入环节,充分的带读和操练使整节课更加实在,使学生能够能动性地学习语言知识点,而不是被动的说教。

阅读环节充分遵循学生学习的规律,采用快读—细读—读后训练的基本模式,且每个阅读环节都能采用不同形式的阅读任务,让完成任务成为学生学习的驱动力,改变传统课堂的以教师为授课主体的形式,真正发挥学生的主观能动性,在完成任务的过程中使得学生的各种阅读技能得到充分的锻炼。阅读后,及时给学生布置任务,对全文及时回顾,并且联系自身,进行内化。在阅读的过程中,教师积极给予适当的指导,尤其是对于阅读技巧方面的指导。

课堂运用了 pair work, group work 等活动,突出了学生学习方式的转变,有效地促进学生积极参与学习的过程。而小组合作互助学习建立在充分的先学基础上,突出了小组互助的力量,强调了学生的学在教学中的重要性。教师在学生合作的时候积极扮演协助者的角色,在学生需要帮助的时候及时给予帮助,适当提醒,让学生能够自己得出答案。并且在学生出错的时候及时纠正。

但是,很多教学细节还有待商榷,学生的表演展示环节由于时间限制,显得过于仓促,应该重新调整课堂节奏,把握课堂重点,给学生充分展示交流的时间。同时,教师在课堂上的教学用语不够精练,应当勤于锤炼,简化指示语,给学生更多的口头表达的机会。另外,板书设计可以进行优化,应当找到板书内容之间的内在联系,使得板书更加具有逻辑性。

点评:

本节课的教学设计安排是由词→句→篇。“词”是基础,“句”是过渡或桥梁,“篇”是目的。整个过程遵循“低起点,小步子”的原则,在步与步之间铺设台阶,构建一个个小的层次,活动的安排由易到难,循序渐进,最后达成目标。准确把握教材重点,突出重点,突破难点。

阅读的过程是首先运用快速阅读这一阅读技巧，设计两个问题让学生总览全文；再次通过细读，设计五个活动内容以锻炼与提升学生的阅读能力；最后设计了复述、完成调查表、两两对话、小组讨论等一系列的读后活动，联系学生的生活实际与自身的经历、知识、观点，激发学生的思维能力、想象能力和创造能力。

本节课的设计还突出强调学生学习方式的转变，通过师生问答、生生对话和小组活动引导学生把接受学习转变为探究学习，把个体学习转变为合作学习。课堂上，教师就是要把课堂还给学生，多让学生来讨论和讲解；把思考空间还给学生，有争议的问题让学生展开讨论，自己找出答案，充分调动学生的学习积极性；把设问质疑还给学生，善于引导学生于无疑处觅有疑，善于激疑并有意训练学生发现问题的能力。如能将以上三点深入到教学的各个环节，本节课的设计会精彩纷呈。

本节课的设计中提到的快速阅读是指利用视觉运动的规律，在较短的时间里阅读文本，从中获得所需信息，使学生提高阅读速度的方法。无论是跳读还是扫读都属于快速阅读的范畴。快速阅读要求运用眼球，扩大视幅，控制视线。阅读表面是用眼睛看，实际是用脑子读。快速阅读可以实现：(1) 通过预测判断文章内容，使思维对新出现的信息有所准备和做出推测，从而促使思维积极活动。(2) 抓主题句，弄清文章的中心论点，准确地预测文章内容。(3) 抓住新信息。阅读是不断获得新信息的过程，弄清文章信息的发展规律，才能构成一个总的概念。(4) 利用学生的竞争心理，用计时阅读训练激发学生的紧迫感和效率意识，总结出“以迅速捕捉信息为目的的速度固定程序”。如果教学设计从这些细节入手会更有新意及实现阅读的有效性。

三、 Grammar 课型

英语语法的理解是对语言结构及语言单位(单词、短语等)在该语言中组合成句的方式的描述,通常包括这些句子在整个语言体系中的意义及功能,它并不一定对语言的语音进行描写。

语法同时又是对说话者语言知识的一种描述。它从语言在说话者心智里是如何组织的以及在说话时运用何种参数的角度去看待语言。

英语语法的表现有形式、语义和语用三个部分。英语语法教学应遵循三个基本原则:隐形语法教学(implicit grammar teaching),即避免直接谈论语法规则,主要通过情景、语言的交际性运用让学生体验语言,归纳出语法规则;意义先行原则(meaning go first),即在一个有意义的情景中理解所教语法项目的意义;提供机会让学生在较真实的语境中运用所学的语法项目进行交际性活动;在前面 meaning 与 use 阶段使用隐形语法教学,在最后面的 form 阶段才采用显性语法教学;适量原则(economy),即讲解语法项目要适时适量,解释清楚即可。学习英语语法的最关键的是体验、认识、再体验、再认识。

(一) Grammar课型特点及设计要求

一、语法教学流程

语法课应根据本模块主题语法知识的学习情况进行合理设计和安排,旨在解决难题,为听说课和读写课的顺利进行铺平道路。

语法教学可以分为体验、归纳、控制性练习和自由运用四个教学环节。体验活动主要是感知语法现象的形式和意义,为归纳语法规则而进行准备。语法的体验可以通过听和读来完成。简单的语法现象,多通过听来感知和体验,在低年级的语法教学中尤其如此。而复杂一些的语法现象,如定语从句等,则多通过阅读来感知和体验。归纳语法规则的活动通常发生在听或读的活动之后,学生通过仔细观察相关的大量语法现象来归纳其中的规则。掌握了规则的用法,学生再通过控制性的练习来验证和运用规则。自由活动是语言的产出活动,注意力完全集中在要表达的内容上面。其过程如下图所示:

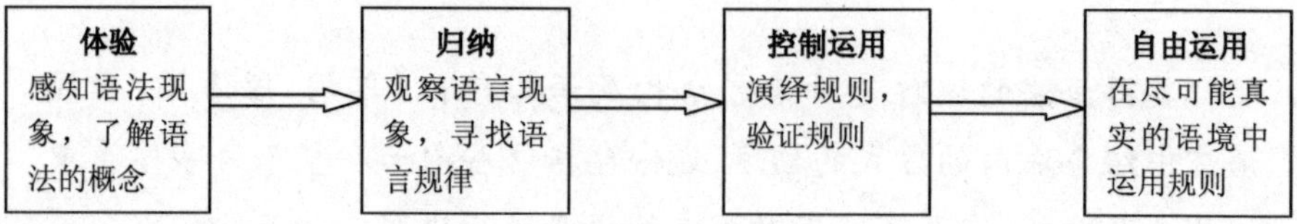

二、环节解读

(一) 复习本节课的相关词汇

引导学生复习与本节课相关的词汇或知识,为新语法项目的顺利学习作铺垫。

(二) 输入新词汇

教师通过创设情境,引出本节课要学的一些新词汇,并通过图片或实物等方式来进行教学,使学生印象深刻,便于记忆。

(三) 语法输入

通过一些典型例句,借助图片、实物、声音等的辅助,来引导学生逐步由浅入深,由易到难,归类、分组地来进行词形变化、人称变化等教学,并及时归纲、练习、小结。突出语法的主要特征,使学生易于接受,乐于接受。

(四) 语法输出

1. 将本节课中涉及的与本节教学内容有关的重点句子罗列到一起,让学生自己从中寻找规律,发现规律,小结用法。

2. 将学生可能寻找出来的语法使用规律通过提问或填空等方式来直接明了地展现给学生,使学生初步掌握并能运用。

(五) 检测与小结

本环节主要通过专项练习来完成。可采取由易到难的形式。"说"的练习建议以学生个人、结对、小组合作等形式进行,"写"的练习可以设计多层次、多种形式的练习,可以先由学生自主完成再结对互评或小组互评。通过学生小组内交流发现问题,先组内解决,不能解决的由教师点拨、指导。

(六) 课后延伸(视学情而定)

(1) 复习巩固。复习当天所学内容,整理课堂笔记,掌握新词汇、语法知识等辅以巩固练习。

（2）分层作业。作业内容可以分层次，分为必做与选做；老师也可以分层次布置内容不同的作业，也可以布置探究性作业，为以后的学习与发展起作用。

（二）Grammar教学设计案例分析

七上 Unit 2 Let's play sports!

Grammar Simple present tense

Background: Simple present tense

It is important for students to master the basic grammar in learning English.

Key words: positive sentence, negative sentence, ask and answer questions

Ⅰ Background information

It is the first tense that students knew and used well in the primary school. However, the students should pay more attention to some key and difficult points. For example, remember that we add "-s" to the verb after he, she or it and some exceptions. Also, they can cultivate some good mental qualities, such as: bravery and confidence. Besides, team spirit and cooperation can be reflected and improved. Last but not least, it is important for students in the middle school to learn by themselves before class.

Ⅱ Type lesson

Grammar lesson

Ⅲ Teaching aims

By the end of the lesson, students should be able to:

1. Master the basic structure of the simple present tense of the verb "to do".
2. Master how to make positive and negative sentences using the verb to do in the simple present tense.
3. Master how to make ask and answer questions using the verb "to do" in the simple present tense.
4. Know when and how to use the simple present tense of the verb "to do".

Ⅳ Teaching content

1. New words and phrases

2. Master the basic structure of the simple present tense of the verb "to do".

3. Master how to make positive and negative sentences using the verb "to do" in the simple present tense.

4. Master how to ask and answer questions using the verb "to do" in the simple present tense.

V Focus of the lesson and predicted area of difficulty

1. New words and phrases

2. The uses of the simple present tense of the verb "to do"

3. Know when and how to use the simple present tense of the verb "to do" freely and correctly

Ⅵ Teaching aids

1. Video	2. Pictures	3. Blackboard	4. Chalk
5. Computer	6. Multimedia	7. Projector	

Ⅶ Teaching procedures

Step 1 *Warm-up and lead-in* (*about 3 – 4 mins.*)

【设计理念：首先，通过观看篮球运动员科比的视频，激发学生学习英语的兴趣并创造一个放松的氛围，更重要的是在与老师的互动过程中让学生说出更多含有行为动词的一般现在时的句子。说出的句子让学生更好地理解行为动词的一般现在时，老师并有意识地用红色粉笔圈出，让学生予以关注，同时也为后面的活动做准备。】

Activity 1: Watch a short video about playing basketball and ask them some questions—Free talk (about 2 – 3 mins.)

Watch a short video about playing basketball and ask them some questions.

T: Boys and girls, let's watch a short video about playing basketball.

Free questions: Ask the students who plays football to introduce the simple present tense of the verb to do.

Do you like this video?

Who plays basketball in the video?

What are they?

They are basketball players. They play basketball very well.

This is Kobe. He is very tall. He looks very strong. (板书，并用红色粉笔将

动词圈出）

Step 2 *Presentation 1—simple present tense（about 5－6 mins.）*

【设计理念：学生周一至周五要上课，生活较单一，通过谈论周末的活动让学生更好地参与课堂。首先，通过老师自身的生活经历来激发学生的话题，调动学生参与的积极性，让学生大胆去说，并爱上用英语交谈；同时在学生说的过程中，老师可以有意识地板书，分人称，且用红色粉笔圈画动词。】

T：They like playing basketball.

What do you like doing?

From Monday to Friday, we don't have much time to play. What about your weekend?

What do you often do at weekends?

（老师可以从自身说起打开话题，呈现图片：I look after my son at weekends. I often take him to the park. I teach him how to sing a song.）

You do homework at the weekend.

He plays volleyball at the weekend.

She goes swimming at weekends.

I go shopping with my friends at weekends.

（在学生回答的过程中，学生都是第一人称回答，老师要有意识地进行追问，引出第二人称和第三人称）

➡Things that we often do.

Simon likes playing football.

➡Things that are true now.

Cats eat fish.

➡Things that are always true.

The sun rises from the east.

Step 3 *Presentation 2（about 6－8 mins.）*

【设计理念：通过给学生创造一个良好的语言环境，同时也为了让学生减少对语法学习的畏惧感，呈现了很多含有行为动词一般现在式的句子，以便于让学生进行归纳总结。】

Activity 1：Presenting—presenting some sentences in this unit with the simple present tense of the verb "to do"(T: In fact, we have learned some sentences like these. We call them the sentences with the simple present tense of the verb "to do")

1. I walk to my bowl many times a day.

2. I like swimming.

3. I often play football.

4. She goes to school every day.

(T: Let's look at them and talk about the structure of them. Write the following on the blackboard.)

I go to school every day.

I don't go to school every day.

Do you go to school every day?

Yes, I do. (No, I don't.)

He goes to school every day.

He doesn't go to school every day.

Does he go to school every day?

Yes, he does. (No, he doesn't.)

***Structures*:**

	I we you they(复数)	*he she it*(单数)
Positive sentences	*sb. + do*	*sb. + does*
Negative sentences	*sb. + don't do*	*sb. + doesn't + do*
Ask and answer sentences	*Do + sb. + do*	*Does + sb. + do*
	Yes, sb. do. *No, sb. don't.*	*Yes, sb. does.* *No, sb. doesn't.*

Activity 2: Rules about how to add an "-s".

Do you want to know how to add an "-s" to the verb? Let's read the table on P23 together. How many ways are there to add an "-s"? What are they?

1. most verbs, 加-s look→looks play→plays

2. most ending in a consonant + y, 去 y 加-ies fly→flies study→studies try→tries carry→carries

3. verbs ending in ch, sh, ss or x, 加-es guess→guesses wash→washes catch→catches mix→mixes

4. some verbs ending in o,加-es go→goes do→does

Sum up the use of adding an "-s" after students' discussion.

(T: You did a good job. We should understand the rules by heart and remember some special changes of words.)

Practice 1: ____________. (写出下列动词的三单形式)

read		fix	
miss		finish	
watch		go	
study		fly	
say		have	
listen		wash	

Practice 2:

【设计理念：通过大量练习的操练,让学生熟知"三单"的用法并正确使用。】

1. He often ________(have) dinner at home.
2. My aunt ________(sing) very well.
3. Linda always ________(go) to school by bike.
4. Mary's friends ________(read) the books every day.
5. My grandma ________(do) morning exercises every morning.

Step 4 *Practice (about 15 - 18 mins.)*

Activity 1: Make sentences and change the sentences.

【设计理念：通过小组活动,激励学生的竞争意识,来更好地掌握行为动词的一般现在时的用法,更好理解其结构并熟练运用。】

T: Let's divide the class into two big groups, Group 1 and Group 2.

Group 1 make a positive sentences with the simple present tense of the verb "to do". Group 2 change the sentences into negative sentences and ask and answer questions.

eg: I want to eat some food now.

I want to eat food and drink water now.

She usually goes shopping at the weekend.

Attention: We do our homework every day.

We do not do our homework every day.

Do you do your homework every day?

Yes, we do.　　No, we don't/do not.

Activity 2: Change the following sentences.

【设计理念：通过习题的操练，让学生掌握含有行为动词一般现在时的肯定句、否定句、一般疑问句、肯否回答及其对画线部分提问。】

1. She does the housework on Sundays.（改为否定句）

2. We have an English lesson every day.（改为一般疑问句）

3. The boy often flies kites.（改为一般疑问句并做否定回答）

4. Does Peter usually go to school by bike?（改为肯定句）

5. They go to the park at weekends.（对画线部分提问）

6. The boys look happy.（对画线部分提问）

Activity 3: Further exercises in the book (about 5 mins.)

【设计理念：这些活动的组织意在让学生学有所获，学有所用。】

Help Millie complete the sentences in Part A with the words in the box. Check the answers.

Step 2 *Presentation*

1. Present negative sentences and ask and answer questions using the verb "to do" in the simple present tense.

2. Finish exercises in Part B. Check the answers.

3. Part C Complete their conversation with the correct forms of the verbs in brackets.

4. Make a dialogue with the deskmates.

Activity 4: Presentation—What does your friend Lily do?

【设计理念：通过大活动的组织和展现，让学生对于掌握较薄弱的动词三单的变化更加关注，并且大胆用英语去说，并在合作过程中体会到快乐学习、快乐分享的成果。】

T: Look and say according to the picture and key words.

(1) Lily, always, on foot

(2) listen, the teachers, carefully(认真地), study, all her lessons

(3) go, park, parents, Sundays

(4) often, help, housework

Step 5 *Homework(about 1 min.)*

【设计理念：通过部分针对性的习题操练，让学生巩固今天课堂所学，也为了更好理解语法规则；拓展性的五句话的家人介绍让学生更好地运用好动词三单的变化规则，也是课堂外的实质性操练和延续。】

(1) Remember the basic structures of the simple present tense of the verb "to do".

(2) Write down five sentences to introduce your family's habits, hobbies or abilities in your exercise book.

(3) Finish a worksheet.

Ⅷ Blackboard design

7A Unit 2　Let's play sports!

Grammar Simple present tense

I/You/We/They like sports.

He/She/It likes sports.

I/You/We/They don't like sports.

He/She/It doesn't like sports.

Do I/you/we/they like sports?

Yes, you/I/we/they do. No, you/I/we/they don't.

Does he/she/it like sports?

Yes, he/she/it does. No, he/she/it doesn't.

Ⅸ Teaching reflection

一般现在时对于学生们来说并不陌生，学生们之前有过大量的句子输入。要想上好这节课，关键在于帮助学生在已知的知识基础上学会归纳总结，课堂上要有一定的新知识生成以及及时的操练和运用。这节课先从一个精彩的篮球视频入手，拉近学生距离，也与本单元的话题相关——让我们做运动吧。接着一步步引导学生们说出关于篮球运动员的相关信息，老师及时板书。然后通过老师周末的活动安排，激发学生谈论他们周末做些什么，通过不同不停的追问，大量的含有一般现在时不同人称的句子出现，学生大量的感知并有意识地进行归纳总结。再让学生说出本节课的语法点，老师通过针对性的习题进行操练。最后通过大活动的组织，鼓励每位学生积极参与，高兴用英语交流，在合作过程中体验成功。

这节课优点在于整节课主线明确，操练具有针对性，语言的大量输入，使得本节课的语法归纳总结水到渠成由学生自己说出。缺点在于：（1）活动设计可以再多样些，比如说设计一些有趣的环节，增加课堂的趣味性。（2）在板书设计一块，可以有更多的形式变化。

点评：

本节语法课打破了传统的授课模式，体现了“不是教授教材，而是用教材教授”的新课程理念。通过观看有关“篮球运动员科比”的录像，激发学生学习英语的兴趣，让学生理解“运动促进健康，运动丰富生活”，从而调动学生学习用一般现在时来描述运动的积极性，这样使学生不再枯燥地学习语法，锻炼了学生的语言实际操作能力，同时也培养学生的体育运动精神，养成坚持不懈和团结协作的良好品质。

教学过程共分 4 大步骤（课程导入、语法讲解、即时操练和家庭作业），采取头脑风暴、分组竞赛等教学方法，开展听、说、读、写的教学活动，围绕课程主题“一般现在时”展开，各个教学活动环环紧扣，训练的侧重点各不相同，但训练综合度逐步提升，在整个教学过程中始终贯穿英语能力训练这条主线。首先通过周末活动比较，让学生在潜移默化中对一般现在时有初步的认识——“避免重复”。再利用表格和例题讲解的形式，条理清晰，帮助学生梳理第三人称单数形式变化，归纳整理重点、难点，易于学生理解和掌握一般现在时。同时穿插“头脑风暴”的方法，扩展学生思维，锻炼了学生的语言实际操作能力。让学生在询问、交流反映过程中进一步练习一般现在时肯定句、否定句和疑问句,最后以看图说话形式综合运用一般现在时,培养孩子连续说英语的能力,体现了学习的最终目的,即学以致用。

七下　Unit 6　Outdoor fun

Grammar　Simple past tense

Background: Outdoor fun

We did a lot of outdoor activities at different time.

Key words: past, activities

Ⅰ　Background information

Students not only study and play at school, but also do a lot of activities outside the school. They enjoy different activities at different time. What about their activities in the past? What did they do?

Ⅱ　Type of the lesson

Grammar lesson

Ⅲ　Teaching aims and learning objectives

By the end of the lesson, the students will be able to:

1. Understand the meanings of the simple past tense.
2. Know the structures of the simple past tense.
3. Grasp the positive and negative sentence structure of the simple past tense.
4. Learn how to ask questions with the simple past tense and answer them.
5. Use the simple past tense to talk about their life.
6. Cooperate with partners and experience the feeling of success.

Ⅳ　Teaching content

1. New words
2. Meanings and structures of the simple past tense
3. Reading, listening, speaking and writing skills

Ⅴ　Focus of the lesson and predicted area of difficulty

1. New words and the story of the sample writing
2. Meanings and structures of the simple past tense
3. Application of the simple past tense

Ⅵ Teaching aids

1. Projector　　2. Multimedia　　3. Blackboard

4. Chalk　　5. Computer

Ⅶ Teaching procedures

Step 1 *The simple past tense—positive sentences(Warm-up and lead-in)*

(1) Present some pictures of what the teacher did last weekend.

【设计理念：1. 用周末外出野营作为切入口，野营时要搭建帐篷导入单词或短语(put up, tent)。2. 用师生对话活跃课堂气氛，提问学生老师周末外出干什么，学生开动脑筋进行猜测，调动了学生参与问题的积极性。3. 周末活动呈现时采用过去时的肯定句式。】

T: What did you do last weekend? What did I do? Guess? Yes, I went out to play with my friends. We went camping in the park. We put up a tent on the grass. I was very happy at that time.

(2) Conclude the structure of the positive sentences.

【设计理念：将导入部分的句式呈现在黑板上，根据这些句式总结过去时肯定式结构，在总结过程中，分为实义动词和 be 动词两类，帮助学生理清两类动词不同的肯定句结构。】

T: Now do you know the structure of positive sentences? Yes, it's "subject + verb(the simple past tense) + other elements", "subject + be(was/were) + other elements".

(3) Practice using the positive structure of the simple past tense.

【设计理念：1. 提问学生周末参加了什么活动，使用一般过去时的肯定句式进行对话，操练一般过去式的肯定句结构。2. 运用肯定句式结构的知识进行实际答题练习。3. 巩固对一般过去式肯定句式结构的理解和记忆。】

T: I did a lot of activities at the weekend. What about you? (找一个学生回答做示范) How about your partners? Talk with your partners (students do pair work). Oh, you really had fun last weekend. But Millie didn't. She did her homework and she had some problems. Can you help her? (练习操练)

Step 2 *The simple past tense—negative sentences*

(1) Present some pictures of what the teacher didn't do last weekend.

【设计理念：通过一些图片告诉老师周末没干哪些事情，呈现出一般过去式的否定句式。分为实义动词和 be 动词两种情况，给学生以初步的直观的感受。】

（2）Conclude the structure of negative sentences.

（设计理念：将由图片导出的句式呈现在黑板上，根据这些句式总结过去时否定句式结构，在总结过程中，分为实义动词和 be 动词两类，帮助学生理清两类动词不同的否定句结构。）

T：Now do you know the structure of negative sentences? Yes, it's "subject + did not + verb + other elements", "subject + be (was/were) + not + other elements".

（3）Practice using the negative structure of the simple past tense.

【设计理念：1. 提问学生及其父母周末没参加什么活动，使用一般过去时的否定句式进行流利对话，操练一般过去时的否定句结构。2. 运用否定句式结构的知识进行实际答题练习。3. 巩固对一般过去时否定句式结构的理解和记忆。】

T：I didn't do many activities at the weekend. What about you?（找一个学生回答做示范）How about your partners? Talk with your partners (students do pair work).

Step 3 *The simple past tense—interrogative sentences*

1. Present some pictures of what the teacher did last weekend.

【设计理念：1. 用师生对话活跃课堂气氛，让两个学生看图问这些人过去做了什么，目的是让学生学会用一般过去时提问题。2. 在黑板上呈现过去时一般疑问句的句子，分 be 动词和实义动词两类。3. 让学生两人一组自己讨论上周末的活动。】

T：What did you do last weekend? Did you do your homework? What else did you do last weekend? What did I do? Guess? Did I go out to play with my friends? Yes, you did. Did we go camping in the park? Did we put up a tent on the grass? Was she very happy at that time? Were we very happy? Yes, you were. Did they have a picnic at that time? No, they didn't.

（2）Conclude the structure of interrogative sentences.

【设计理念：将导入部分的句式呈现在黑板上，根据这些句式总结过去时疑问句式结构，在总结过程中，分为实义动词和 be 动词两类，帮助学生理清两

类动词不同的疑问句结构,并且做肯定和否定回答。】

T: Now do you know the structure of interrogative sentences? Yes, it's "did/was were + subject + verb (the simple present tense) + other elements".

(3) Practice using the interrogative structure of the simple past tense.

【设计理念: 1. 提问学生周末参加了什么活动,使用一般过去时的疑问句式进行对话,操练一般过去时的疑问句结构。2. 运用疑问句式结构的知识进行实际答题练习。3. 巩固对一般过去时疑问句式结构的理解和记忆。】

T: (找一个学生回答做示范) Did you do housework last weekend? Yes/No. What else did you do last weekend? I did ... (找两个学生对话) How about your partners? Talk with your partners (students do pair work).

Step 4 *Homework*

【设计理念: 1. 在小组合作的基础上,开始个人写作,巩固课堂所学。2. 引导对写作感兴趣的同学,进行自己创作、改编。】

T: Now please remember your homework:

(1) Write the story by yourself and share it with each other.

(2) Choose one of your favorite novels (小说) and try to write more about it.

Ⅷ Blackboard design

7B Unit 6 Outdoor fun

Grammar Simple past tense

New words: put up, a tent

The simple past tense:

肯定: subject + V (the simple past tense)/be (was/were) + ...

否定: subject + didn't + V (the simple present tense) + ...

subject + was not/were not + ...

疑问句: Did subject + do ... ?

Yes, ... did.

No, ... did not.

Was/Were sb. ... ?

Yes, ... was/were.

No, ... wasn't/weren't.

Ⅸ Teaching reflection

本节课主要处理语法一般过去时，分为肯定句结构、否定句结构和一般疑问句结构。肯定句导入时运用周末情境，周末外出做什么活动，呈现肯定句结构。呈现过程中有意识引导学生注意两类动词：行为动词和 be 动词。然后总结规则，并进行口语操练，让学生运用肯定句结构描述过去做过的事情。学生对开头的导入十分感兴趣，因为这是与学生生活息息相关的。否定句导入时也是运用周末情境，通过几幅图片导出周末老师没参加哪些活动，呈现否定句结构。呈现过程中有意识引导学生注意两类动词：行为动词和 be 动词。然后总结规则，让学生两两对话谈论他们及其父母周末没做什么活动，进行一般过去时否定句式的操练，让学生运用否定句结构描述过去没有做过的事情。疑问句的导入主要是让学生自己说出过去时疑问句的句子，自己训练这样的句子，所以让两个学生看着图片问问题比较重要，要分 be 动词和实义动词两类句子问，分别总结规律。让学生做一个完整对话也很好地锻炼了学生使用过去时的能力。同时顺带复习一下特殊疑问词的使用以及疑问句的肯定回答和否定回答。在疑问句的学习部分，老师一定要注意的是，自己不要问太多问题，不要说太多话，引导学生自问自答。

点评：

本节课语法教学设计让学生在语境中进行语法教学，不是孤立地、死板地记住一些语法规则。活动有明确的交际目的和真实的交流意义，即向同学们介绍自己的一次周末活动。这些活动的层次性强，操作要求具体，指导性强。学生先听别人讲述自己的一次周末活动，了解干了什么，没有干什么，这有利于内化语言知识，发现语法规则。接下来，学生通过小组合作，不断进行细节追问，达成一般过去时三种结构的现实操练。之后，同伴之间相互转述朋友的一次周末活动，培养学生连续说英语的能力。教师为学生使用目的语提供了有用的支持。学习的活动内容和形式都贴近学生的生活实际，符合学生的认知水平和生活经验。在这些活动中，语法的学习以一种渗透的方式进行，即学生在交流思想的过程中掌握语法，学习语法的过程变得比较有趣和比较有意义，优化了英语学习方式。

这个案例说明语法的学习不一定非要教师仔仔细细地讲解，学生可以从语言输入中观察到语言的规律性东西，观察到这些规律只是语言学习的第一步，还要进一步在情境中运用巩固。通过运用，帮助学生内化语言规则。

八上 Unit 4 Do it yourself

Grammar

Giving instructions, using "should" and "had better"

Background

DIY cards and advice

Ⅰ Background information

When people DIY, they need to understand the instructions and follow them. Thus, they need to get a good knowledge of how to read instructions and how to give them, so that they will be able to know how to DIY and what to do. Among all the instructions and advice, knowing and telling others what they think is the best or right thing to do are important too.

Ⅱ Type of the lesson

Grammar lesson

Ⅲ Teaching aims and learning objectives

By the end of the lesson, the students will be able to:

1. Understand the meanings of the new words and use them in proper situations.
2. Use the imperative sentences to give instructions.
3. Use "should" and "had better" to give advice.
4. Know how to do a DIY job and teach others to do it.
5. Learn to work in groups and share with each other.

Ⅳ Teaching content

1. New words
2. Use the imperative sentences to give instructions
3. Should and had better

Ⅴ Focus of the lesson and predicted area of difficulty

1. The imperative sentences
2. How to use "should" and "had better"

Ⅵ Teaching aids

1. DIY tools　2. Blackboard　3. Chalk

4. Computer　5. Multimedia　6. Projector

Ⅶ Teaching procedures

Step 1 *Tools and usages (Warm-up and lead-in)*

Show DIY tools and ask students to describe their usages.

【设计理念：1. 利用 DIY 工具引导学生复习已学知识，用 scissors 导入生词 cut。2. 引导学生造句表达，导入生词 sentence。3. 使用祈使句表达工具用途，用祈使句否定形式表达使用工具的注意事项。4. 通过实物展示，用师生对话活跃课堂气氛，调动学生参与的积极性。】

T：We learned a lot about DIY and DIY tools. Do you know these tools?

What can they do?（展示工具）

Please tell us like this sentence：Use the scissors to cut paper.（引导学生使用祈使句肯定形式）

But sometimes we have to be careful with these tools. For example, don't play with scissors. What else?（引导学生使用祈使句否定形式）

Step 2 *Work out the rule*

【设计理念：1. 在导入环节之后，学生有了知识铺垫。采用小组合作形式，学生联系新旧知识，自己总结祈使句的结构和用法等。2. 利用小组活动，调动课堂气氛，促进学生自主学习祈使句，变被动接受为主动学习。3. 讲解祈使句用法。】

T：Read these sentences. Can you find the structure of the sentences?（通过小组讨论，学生自主学习发现祈使句的结构）

From the sentences, when do we use the imperative sentences?（启发学生发现祈使句用于给予指令）

Let's find more about the imperative sentences.（在学生已经认知的基础上，教师讲解祈使句及其用法）

Step 3 *Practice*

【设计理念：1. 通过书本练习，操练用祈使句给予指令，强化所学内容，让学生会说、会用。2. 通过快速反应游戏，让学生运用所学谈论生活中的指示牌等，拓展加深所学内容，并活跃课堂气氛。】

T：Just now we got to know how to use the tools. Let's DIY a card! Can you give us any instructions?（通过创设活动情境，让学生使用所学内容，完成书本

练习）

Great! Can I make a beautiful card if I follow your instructions? What shouldn't we do? Do you have any instructions?（延伸书本上的练习，引导学生使用祈使句的否定形式）

OK, besides DIY, we can give many other instructions in our daily life. Let's check who knows most.（利用生活中的许多指示标牌等，让学生快速反应，强化对祈使句的理解和实际运用）

Step 4 *Group work*

【设计理念：1. 学生通过共同完成小组任务，学会灵活运用祈使句。2. 让学生自己想出校园生活中应该注意的事项，将所学内容拓展延伸，并在课堂中施予学生情感教育。3. 利用学生展示的内容为下一环节 should/had better 做好铺垫。】

T: We should follow these instructions in our life. What instructions should we follow at school? Can you give us any instructions?

（分组进行讨论在校园生活中要注意哪些事项，让学生用祈使句表达出来）

Each group has different focuses. Please discuss and write them down. Remember to use the imperative sentences.

I want some of you to show your instructions to us.

Step 5 *Should/Had better (Lead-in)*

【设计理念：1. 利用上一个小组活动中学生说到的句子，导入 should 和 had better。2. 使学生联系起已学内容，为进一步学习做好准备。】

T: You give us a lot of instructions. So we should listen carefully in class.（举其中一个例子）What else should we do?（引导学生使用 should do sth.）

What shouldn't we do?

So, we had better do ...

We had better not do ...

（教师引导学生尝试用 should/shouldn't, had better/had better not 表达建议）

Step 6 *Work out the rule*

【设计理念：1. 在导入环节之后，学生有了知识铺垫。采用小组合作形式，学生联系新旧知识，自己总结 should 和 had better 用法等。2. 利用小组活动，调动课堂气氛，促进学生自主学习祈使句，变被动接受为主动学习。3. 讲解祈使句用法。】

T：Read these sentences. Can you find how to use "should" and "had better"?（通过小组讨论，学生自主学习总结 should/had better 用法）

When do we use "should" and "had better"?

Let's find more about the usages of "should" and "had better".（在学生已经认知的基础上，教师讲解用法）

Step 7 *Practice*

【设计理念：1. 通过书本练习，操练用 should/had better 给予建议，强化所学内容，让学生会说会用。2. 设置 pair work 活动，学生通过两两对话，在锻炼听说能力的同时，拓展加深所学内容。】

T：When we do DIY jobs, we need to follow instructions. And we had better take some good advice. Can you give us any advice?（通过创设活动情境，让学生使用所学内容，完成书本练习）

Great! Suzy and her classmates are talking about DIY advice. Can you help them complete the dialogue?（延伸书本上的练习，引导学生使用 should, had better 和 It's better to do，通过 pair work 对话强化语言运用）

Step 8 *Group work*

【设计理念：1. 要求学生共同完成小组任务，促进学生灵活运用本节课所学内容。2. 鼓励学生积极动手，用英语表达指令和建议。3. 通过小组合作让学生学会合作和分享。】

T：During this year's English festival, we will have a Christmas present DIY. Now, what do you want to DIY?

Here are some choices. Please choose one from them, discuss how to DIY it and give some advice on your DIY job with group members.

Remember to use what we learnt in this lesson.

Let's show your instructions and advice.

Step 9 *Homework*

【设计理念：1. 完善最后一个任务。2. 巩固课堂所学。】

T：Now please remember your homework：

(1) Make your instructions and advice better.

(2) Do some exercises.

Ⅷ Blackboard design

8A Unit 4 Do it yourself—Grammar

Use scissors to cut.

Make sentences.

Don't play with scissors.

Give instructions：

The imperative sentence：Do sth. /Don't do sth.

Please do sth. /Please don't do sth.

If you … , you will …

Give advice：

should/should not do sth.

had better do sth. /had better not do sth.

It's better for sb. (not) to do sth.

Ⅸ Teaching reflection

在本节语法课中，主要通过 DIY 相关话题学习给予指令和提供建议，学会正确使用祈使句以及 should 和 had better 这两个用法。学生在本课教授之前，对于祈使句以及 should 和 had better 已经有相关的知识铺垫，因此，本课主要侧重知识的梳理归纳以及灵活运用。本课在 DIY 这一情境下，以 DIY 活动为主线，分两部分分别教学。

第一部分导入部分就运用课本所创设的 DIY 情境，引导学生使用祈使句表达 DIY 工具的用途以及使用时的注意事项，将祈使句肯定句和否定句分别依次导入，引导学生多说。如此，既可以联系旧知识，为新知识做好铺垫，又可以达到活学活用，活跃课堂的目的。第二部分则是利用上一部分的操练，将两部分知识联系起来。两部分呈现以及讲授都是借助小组合作的形式，倡导学生自主、合作学习。学生积极参与讨论，主动梳理总结已经学过的相关知识，并能自主学习本课新知识。

对于所学内容的操练，并没有局限于书本，而是将书本练习融入课堂环节中。对于活动的设计也没有局限于 DIY 这一话题，引入了学生所熟悉的其他话题，例如，学校生活注意事项以及英语节活动。

但是，本课也存在问题，对于所学内容的深化和拓展有些局限于本单元，再者设计活动集中在说和读，听和写较为缺乏，教师在备课时需要更加全面的考虑。

点评：

该案例依据《标准（2011 年版）》中听的四级目标要求和学习策略五级的目标要求，按照“语言接触——理解体验——语言聚焦——自主运用”的教学思路，对本节课的教学进行设计，确立了四个教学环节：复习导入、语言输入、语言聚焦和语言运用。

在复习导入环节，教师以回答问题的形式复习 DIY 工具，表达工具用途，用祈使句否定形式说明使用工具的注意事项，为本节课的学习打基础。

在语言输入环节，教师通过小组讨论，学生自主学习祈使句结构，引导学生通过祈使句发出指令，并以快速反应游戏，来活跃课堂气氛；在语言聚焦环节，教师引导学生通过观察、发现和归纳，聚焦祈使句的构成和意义，并利用校园生活注意事项进行语言操练，并引导学生尝试用 should(not), had better(not)表达建议；在语言运用环节，教师创设贴近学生生活的语言情境，引导学生运用所学的语言，达到学以致用的目的。

到本节课结束时，所有学生都用祈使句及两个句型发出指令，给出建议，达成了本课所制订的教学目标。

八下　Unit 7　International charities

Grammar Passive Voice

Background: Passive voice

Students have a new way to perform the action.

Key words: passive voice in the simple present and past tenses

I　Background information

Students have met passive voice before. For example, I was trapped. (8A Unit 8 Reading) However, we didn't ask students to pay attention to it. It's an important grammar for students to express the action that is more important than the person who performs the action.

Ⅱ Type of the lesson

Grammar lesson

Ⅲ Teaching aims and learning objectives

By the end of the lesson, students should be able to:

1. Master the basic structure of passive voice.
2. Master the uses of passive voice in the simple present tense.
3. Master the uses of passive voice in the simple past tense.
4. Know when and how to use passive voice.
5. Master how to change a sentence from active voice to passive voice.

Ⅳ Teaching content

1. New phrases
2. Passive voice in the simple present and past tenses

Ⅴ Focus of the lesson and predicted area of difficulty

1. New phrases
2. The uses of passive voice
3. How to change a sentence from active voice to passive voice

Ⅵ Teaching aids

1. Video 2. Pictures 3. Blackboard 4. Chalk
5. Computer 6. Multimedia 7. Projector

Ⅶ Teaching procedures

Step 1 *Warm-up and lead-in* (*about 3 -5 mins.*)

【设计理念:通过播放英文歌曲,为学生创造一种学习英语的氛围。激发学生学习兴趣。通过谈论英语歌曲的自由对话,自然导入被动语态,同时呈现一般现在时态和一般过去时态的被动语态,为下一步详细呈现做好铺垫。】

Activity 1: Listen to an English song called "My heart will go on" and ask them to sing together——Free talk(about 3 -5 mins.)

Play and ask the students to listen to the song "My hear will go on" and ask them to sing together.

T: Boys and girls, let's listen to an English song called "My hear will go on" and try to sing together.

Free questions: Ask the students who sing this song to introduce active voice and passive voice.

Do you like this song?

Who sings this song?

Who sang this song just now?

Celine Dion sings this song.

This song is sung by Celine Dion.

We sang this song just now.

This song was sung by us just now.

Step 2 *Presentation (about 8 – 12 mins.)*

Activity 1: Presenting—presenting some sentences in this unit with passive voice in the simple present tense and the simple past tense.

【设计理念：呈现出我们在本单元的 Reading 部分刚刚学的含有被动语态的句子，一方面可以减少学生对新语法知识的恐惧感，另一方面学生对这些句子已经很熟悉，学生易于快速理解句意。】

(T: In fact, we have learned some sentences like these. We call them the sentences with passive voice.)

1. About 80 per cent of these cases can be prevented or cured.

2. The plane is also used as a training center.

3. Local doctors and nurses are invited on board to learn about eye operations.

4. During my last visit, 150 patients were operated on.

5. Most eye problems and diseases can be treated and cured. But more money is needed to carry on with our work.

Activity 2: Present the structures of passive voice in the simple present tense and the simple past tense.

【设计理念：通过刚刚大家熟悉的一般现在时态和一般过去时态的两个句子，呈现由主动语态变为被动语态的方法，减少同学们对新学语法的恐惧心理，将语法学习放到真实语境中，让学生易于接受新知。】

(T: Let's look at them and talk about the structure of them. Write the following on the blackboard.)

Structures of passive voice in the simple present tense and the simple past tense:

passive voice in the simple present tense:

The object in the active voice + am/is/are + done + by the subject in the active voice.

passive voice in the simple past tense:

The object in the active voice + was/were + done + by the subject in the active voice.

The difference is: We change the subject in the active voice into the object in the passive voice with "by" before it. We also change the verb in the active voice into its the past participle form.

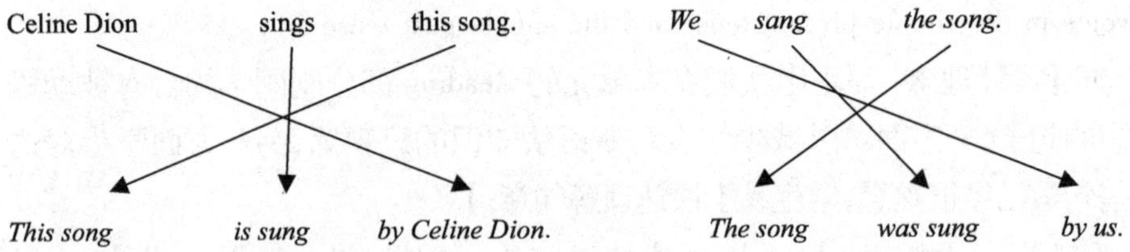

Activity 3: Discussion

Show students more sentences, asking them to find out the differences among the sentences with passive voice. At last, try to discuss how to use "by" correctly.

【设计理念：通过例句和讨论，让学生感受一般现在时态和一般过去时态的被动语态的句子，在语境中理解"by"的用法。】

The cake was eaten by Daniel.

The little dog is looked after very well by Simon.

The computer is bought by my uncle.

I am woken up by my father every morning.

The trees are planted in March.

The computers are widely used.

The tall buildings were built last year.

The thief was caught yesterday.

Sum up the use of "by" after students' discussion.

(T: You did a good job. We can introduce who or what performs an action in the passive voice using "by". Sometimes, if we don't know or we don't need to tell others who or what performs an action in the passive voice, we often omit "by".)

Step 3 *Practice(about 15 – 18 mins.)*

Activity 1: Choose the sentences in passive voice.

【设计理念：通过提供例句让学生学会辨别被动语态的句子，在辨别中强化学生对被动语态结构的记忆，避免单调的语法条目灌输，让学生在语境中理解被动语态。】

T: Please make a tick "√" before the sentences in passive voice. (about 2 mins.)

1) The meeting lasted 3 hours yesterday. (　　)

2) We have lunch at 12 o'clock. (　　)

3) Homework is done by Daniel every evening. (　　)

4) 300 trees were planted by us yesterday. (　　)

5) Classroom is cleaned every day. (　　)

6) The students in China learn English at school. (　　)

Activity 2: Change the following sentences in active voice into the sentences in passive voice. (about 10 – 12 mins.)

【设计理念：通过提供学生一些例句，让学生在主动语态和被动语态相互转换的实践中探索和学会这两种语态的转换方法，达到让学生体会学以致用的教学目的。】

(1) On the plane, volunteer doctors do operations.

(2) ORBIS doctors improve the lives of patients.

(3) We plant trees.

(4) ORBIS doctors helped many blind people.

(5) Many people speak English.

(6) They built a new bridge over the river.

(7) Farmers grow rice in China.

(8) He published this book in 2003.

(9) A policeman saved the little girl.

Activity 3: Further exercise in the certain background. (about 8 mins.)

【设计理念：通过处理书本练习，在图片创设的语境中集中练习将一般现在时态的主动语态句子变为被动语态句子的方法，让学生及时总结方法。】

T：The Class 1, Grade 8 students are talking about the different things people can do for the poor. Look at the pictures and help them complete their notes using the words in brackets and the passive voice. Add the word "by" when necessary.

T：What do they do every year?

1. Charity activities ____________________(plan/to help the poor).

2. Leaflets ____________________(hand out/to people in the street/volunteers).

3. Toys and CDs ____________________(sell/to raise money).

T：When we change the sentences in active voice into the sentences in passive voice, we should keep the same tense.

Activity 3：Further exercise in the same background. (about 4 mins.)

【设计理念：通过处理书本练习，在本单元话题下的图片创设出的语境中集中练习将一般过去时态的主动语态句子变为被动语态句子的方法，让学生及时总结方法。老师通过学生的完成情况了解学生本节课的学习情况。】

T：What did they do last week?

4 new books ____________________(send/to children in poor areas/the Class 1, Grade 8 students).

Warm clothes ____________________(collect/for poor people).

A charity show ____________________(hold/the Students' Union).

Activity 4：Amy and Daniel are talking about charities. Complete their conversation with the words in brackets using the passive voice.

【设计理念：通过书本上提供的情境，完成 Amy 和 Daniel 的对话，综合地训练学生将一般现在时态和一般过去时态的句子转化成被动语态句子的能力，使学生在适当的训练中能力得到提升。】

Amy：I'm reading a book about Oxfam.

Daniel：Really? Please tell me about it.

Amy：OK. Oxfam ________(set up) in the UK in 1942, and the first Oxfam shop ________(open) in 1948. Now it has about 15,000 shops in all over the world. A lot of things ________(sell) in Oxfam shops, including books. The money ________(use) by Oxfam to help poor people.

Daniel：That's good. There are also some charity projects in China. One of them ________(call) Project Hope. It ________(start) in 1989. With its help, millions of poor children all over the country ________(give) basic education.

Step 4 *Homework*

【设计理念：通过让学生记忆两种时态的被动语态结构，使学生总结本节课所学语法的规则，并利用这些规则将一些句子转化成被动语态，以达到巩固所学知识的目的。】

(1) Remember the basic structures of the passive voice in the simple present tense and in the simple past tense.

(2) Change more sentences in the active voice in Reading into the passive voice.

Ⅷ Blackboard design

Unit 7 International charities

Grammar

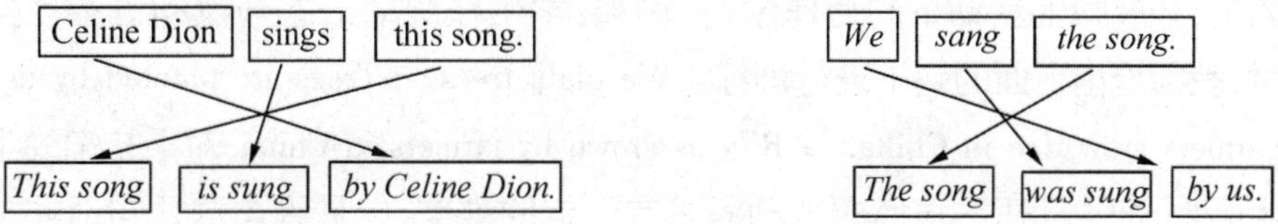

The passive voice in the simple present tense:

The object in the active voice + am/is/are + done + by the subject in the active voice.

passive voice in the simple past tense：

Object in the active voice + was/were + done + by Subject in the active voice.

Ⅸ Teaching reflection

这节课优点在于：首先，课堂从一首英语歌曲导入，学生很轻松且拥有较好的情感进入到英语课堂中来。其次，教师将新学的语法放到具体的情境中去呈现和练习，而不是单纯地灌输单调的变化规则。最后，老师所举事例贴近学生生活和学生的当前认知水平，学生易于理解和接受。

有待改进的方面：老师没有着重呈现一般现在时态的被动语态和一般过去时态的被动语态的区别，没有培养和树立学生学习语态的时态观，这可能为学生以后学习其他时态的被动语态带来一些困难。

点 评：

本案例旨在帮助学生通过对主动语态和被动语态的比较，明白主语和动词之间的关系以确定动词该使用主动语态还是被动语态，并且能够通过本课的学习学会触类旁通，更好地学习不同时态的被动语态。

在设计上，先以 Celine Dion 演唱的 My heart will go on 视频导入新课。振奋人心的歌曲立即把学生的注意力集中起来。以歌曲为切入点导入被动语态：This song is sung by Celine Dion. Her songs are liked by many people. 这样的导入很自然、开门见山，为后面的学习起了很好的铺垫作用。接下来由所学被动语态的几个句子引出被动语态这一概念，然后再对这一概念进行讲解（包括定义、结构、何时运用），通过图示法让学生学习掌握各种时态的被动语态，通过让学生辨别、对比主动语态和被动语态的句子，引导学生学会判断主语和动词的关系，确定动词使用何种语态来表达，再通过不同形式的练习巩固所学知识，有头脑风暴、小组讨论等，学生学习的积极性高、参与欲强、参与面广。

本案例在被动语态教学中，是这样尝试组织和运用合作学习的：以学生为主，开展师生互动下的合作学习，例如，学生在主动语态与被动语态互换时，教师给出下面的句子进行训练。We plant trees. →Trees are planted by us. Farmers grow rice in China. → Rice is grown by farmers in China. 对于初学的学生而言，把主动语态转换成被动语态有一定的难度，但是因为这几句话非常贴近生活，学生在合作中能够加深对被动语态的理解，掌握两者转换的方法，老师只要简洁地点拨一下，学生就能很好地掌握被动语态了。

九上 Unit 2 Colours

Grammar

Objective clauses introduced by "that", "if" or "whether"

I Background information

To the students of Grade Nine, the object clause is not an unfamiliar grammatical phenomenon. Before this lesson, students have contacted some simple object clauses such as I know that ... I think that and so on. But it is difficult for students to master the rules for the use of the object clause. Most of them are curious about the object clauses and desire to fully clarify them. Moreover, the grammar is set in the knowledge of the relationship between colors and moods.

II Type of the lesson

Grammar lesson

III Teaching aims and learning objectives

By the end of the lesson, the students will be able to:

1. Know what is the object clause.
2. Learn the object clause introduced by "that".
3. Learn the object clauses introduced by "if" or "whether".
4. Learn to change and use object clauses in the right context.
5. Increase their interest and set up self-confidence in language study by completing the task.

IV Teaching content

1. New words
2. The object clause introduced by "that", "if" or "whether"

V Focus of the lesson and predicted area of difficulty

1. Learn to use "that", "if" or "whether" correctly.
2. Know the words which can be put before the object clause.
3. Learn the right word order in the object clause.

VI Teaching aids

1. Blackboard 2. Chalk 3. Computer 4. Multimedia
5. Projector

Ⅶ Teaching procedures

Step 1 *Revision and lead-in*

Give some pictures of colors and moods and talk about them.

【设计理念：1. 在一些与颜色、情绪相关知识的背景下，导入单词或短语(everyday, personal taste)，让学生在上下文语境中理解记忆生词。2. 通过添加乐嘉的性格色彩学说来拓展学生的知识面，激起学生的兴趣。】

T：Boys and girls, look at the pictures and think about what we have learnt in Reading.

T：Yes! The article tells us that colors influence our everyday mood.（板书整句话并带读 everyday）

T：Different people like different colors. They have their own personal taste.（板书带读 personal taste）

T：What color do you like best?

T：Some people believe that there is a relationship between colours and personalities.（板书整句话）

Step 2 *The object clause introduced by "that"*

(1) Definition：What is the object?

【设计理念：通过给出例句，遵循由特殊到一般的知识习得规律，让学生思考语法规则，利于记忆。】

T：OK. Now tell me what part this sentence is in this complexed sentence.

T：Yes. It functions as the object of a sentence. So it is an object clause.

(2) Sum up rules：How to make an object clause.

【设计理念：通过例句总结宾语从句使用规则，再由一般到特殊，给出一些例句让学生体会如何使用宾语从句。】

T：And we use "that" to introduce an object clause that is a statement. For example, "Colors influence our everyday mood" is a statement.

T：An object clause can be put after verbs such as know, think, believe, hope and mean.

T：An object clause can also follow adjectives such as certain, sure and glad. For example, "He is glad that the walls in his room are blue."（板书分两类

a. 动词 b. 形容词)

Tips: In informal English we often drop that.

(3) Practise

【设计理念:通过相关练习巩固操练学生对 that 引导的宾语从句的掌握。练习由易到难,层次逐渐提高。】

T: Here are some sentences. Now try to tell whether they are object clauses.

a. These planets will produce food and oxygen that we need to live on Mars.

b. Scientists will develop plants that can grow on Mars.

c. People think that humans on Mars have to wear special boots to make themselves heavier.

d. You may wonder whether colors influence our moods.

T: Let's check the answers.

Step 3 *The object clauses introduced by "if" or "whether"*

(1) Presentation

【设计理念:通过上面练习中出现的一个例句引导学生发现其与所学宾语从句的区别,鼓励学生独立思考,不至于老师全权包办。】

T: Now look at last sentence. It's also an object clause. What's the difference between this object clause and other object clauses? (板书 You may wonder whether colors influence our moods. 这句话并且找一个学生回答)

T: The other object clauses uses "that" to connect two sentences while this sentence uses "whether" to connect two sentences.

(2) Sum up rules: How to make an object clause introduced by "if" or "whether".

【设计理念:给出例句使学生总结 if/whether 引导的宾语从句。】

T: We use "if" or "whether" to introduce an object clause that expresses a yes/no question. Such an object clause often follows verbs such as "ask", "see", and "wonder".

T: The sentence "You may wonder whether colors influence our moods" is made up of "You may wonder" and "Do colors influence our moods?" The word order in the clause should be the same as that in a statement. For example, Sandy asks if/whether orange can cheer her up.

(3) Practise

【设计理念：通过操练来巩固强化学生对 if/whether 引导的宾语从句的练习，if 和 whether 引导的宾语从句的语序问题是本节课的重难点，通过连接句子能很好地提高学生对这块知识的敏感度。】

T：Here are some exercises. Now please connect two sentences with object clauses.

a. They wonder

Will Miss Li be in charge of their class?

b. Do you remember

Has he entered the contest?

c. I ask him

Do you often come here to read newspapers?

d. I want to know

Is he a League member?

T：Let's check the answers.

Step 4 *Consolidate*

(1) To make sentences with object clauses introduced by "*that*", "*if*" or "*whether*".

【设计理念：通过图片形象地将 if/whether/that 糅在一起操练巩固学生对定语从句的掌握。】

a. What did the cat think?

I want something to eat.

b. What did Ted ask Jane?

Can you lend your pen to me?

c. Has my father got any fish?

What does the baby cat ask?

d. We all know

The West Lake is very famous in the world.（幻灯片呈现与句子匹配的图片，让四位同学回答）

(2) Chain work (Describe something or ask something about object clauses learnt in this lesson)

【设计理念：1. 通过学生之间的合作创造真实的情景来巩固操练本节课所学的 if，whether 或者 that 引导的宾语从句，这样的操练使得学生对宾语从句的理解更加具体，从而使用起来更加熟练，而不是抽象的练习题训练。2. 培养学生的合作意识并提高合作能力。提高课堂气氛，让相对沉闷的语法知识焕发活力。增强学生的学习兴趣。3. 为 group work 铺垫。】

T：If one student asks the student behind him or her one question，the third student will describe their conversation with object clauses. If one student describes his or her idea，the second student will tell others what his or her idea is.（找两排展示）

（3）Group work：Write a composition（Who can use the most object clauses?）

【设计理念：在颜色的情境中进行当堂反馈，让学生先在组内讨论再使用 if，whether 或者 that 引导的宾语从句写一篇 80 字左右的文章，能够扩大学生的参与面，提高学生的英语语言组织能力。】

T：Now we have learnt something about colors. Please use object clauses introduced by "that"，"if" or "whether" as much as possible to write a composition. Work in groups.

T：OK，now let's see which group has the most object clauses.（找两组呈现作文）

（4）Proverbs：Show some proverbs concerning colors.

【设计理念：通过英文谚语，升华主题，启发学生对颜色的兴趣。】

Step 5 *Homework*

【设计理念：通过这样的作业培养学生及时巩固复习所学知识的好习惯。】

T：Now please take down your homework：

a. Revise the contents we've learned in Grammar.

b. Recite some key words，phrases & sentences mentioned in Grammar.

c. Pre-learn integrated skills.

Ⅷ Blackboard design

9A Unit 2 Colors—Grammar

Objective clauses introduced by "that"，"if" or "whether"

Object clauses introduced by "that"

The article tells us that colors influence our everyday mood.

Some people believe that there is a relationship between colors and personalities. (after verbs)

He is glad that the walls in his room are blue. (after adjectives)

Object clauses introduced by "whether" or "if"

You may wonder whether/if colors influence our moods.

the word order in a statement

Ⅸ Teaching reflection

本课在设计时突出体现了理解所学语法项目并能在特定语境中使用的语法课教学目标。通过接触、理解、操练、运用语言等环节，逐步实现语言知识的内化。在导入时就通过与颜色相关的图片激发学生兴趣，在这个环节谈论的又是他们熟悉的事物，学生的兴趣继续得到激发，更能使师生之间的互动变得生动活泼起来。通过这个环节让学生尝试自我总结语法规则，老师在整个过程中起到的只是一种抛砖引玉的作用，也不用担心学生犯错：要让学生学会自我纠错，学生的自我纠错更能体现教学的有效性是否得到体现。

紧接着回归课本，夯实基础，对课本上的基础练习进行一个简单的练习和讲解，巩固基本知识点。之后再给出一些能力提高的练习，这个环节对学生提出了更高的能力上的要求，也更能检验出学生是否已掌握该知识点。此外，本环节还为下面的环节铺垫，使得课堂更加的连贯。

教学流程遵循由特殊到一般再由一般到特殊的认知规律，使得学生对本节课知识的掌握呈螺旋式上升，帮助学生更好地掌握新知识。

课堂一些环节的设计是基于学生合作的形式，运用了 chain work，group work 等活动，体现了"自主、合作、探究"的理念，强调语言学习的实践性，主张学生在语境中接触语法点，体验和理解语言使用规则，并在此基础上学习和运用语言。小组合作等形式有效地调动学生参与课堂的积极性，教师因势利导，使学生通过亲身体验产生学习兴趣并获得成功。

但是，很多教学细节还有待修改完善。Step Seven 环节由于指示语不明确导致学生在课堂上不知所措，影响了课堂效率，使得预期效果大打折扣。作为年轻老师，对课堂的调动掌握还有待提高。学习评价的自主权可以再适当放手，让学生参与评价。

点评:

本案例是一节符合语法教学规律的很实在的常态课。能以色彩、情绪为教学主线;以乐嘉的性格色彩学说来导入并激发学生的兴趣;以与 Reading 相关的重点句子来板书、分析;遵循由特殊到一般再由一般到特殊的认知规律,让学生思考语法规则,体会如何使用宾语从句;以紧扣主题的活动师生互动、生生互动使课堂活泼起来,让学生尝试自我总结语法规则,有力提高训练实效。本案例思路清晰,条理性好,能按照教学内容要求,循序渐进,一步一步把教学目标落实到位,正是这根清晰的教学主线将所有的课堂活动有机地联系起来。这是本课的亮点。本课给人特别深刻的印象:很注重每个知识点的展和收,每一个环节结束总是及时总结,给学生记忆和思考的空间。

课堂教学设计是教学改革向纵深发展的产物,它改变教师的教学行为,它与传统教案的主要区别可以归纳为两点:一是要对学习者(学生)的特征进行分析,关注学生的现有认知能力、知识结构特点和特定知识,以明确课堂教学的起点。二是学习内容分析,要关注课堂教学知识点的划分、各知识点之间的逻辑关系以及与相邻知识点之间的联系,形成知识网络,养成从整体看局部的思维习惯。

四、 Integrated skills 课型

Integrated skills(综合技能)板块在译林版《牛津初中英语》(Fun with English)在单元话题下安排的各个板块中,是最具特色的一个部分。

该板块将语言结构和交际功能相结合,学生应在所设计的情景中学习使用与本单元主题相关的交际用语,并能把所学的交际用语灵活自然地运用到日常生活情境中。

(一) Integrated skills 课型特点及设计要求

Integrated skills 板块由听力部分和口头训练部分组成,听力部分培养学生从听力原文中获取信息、处理信息和使用信息的能力;口头训练部分以对话形式呈现一些有用的句式或地道的表达方法,供学生模仿练习。其目的是以听说为主,辅以简单的阅读和少量的写的练习,从而从听、说、读、写四个方面全方位地对学生加以训练。

1. 听前的活动设计(Pre-listening)

为激活学生已有的相关知识,增加学生的相关文化和背景知识,扫除生词障碍,并预测听力材料的内容及结构,为听力教学做好铺垫。老师要尽可能选择学生熟悉的、了解的或感兴趣的内容,通过图片、对话、视频等形式,激发学生听的欲望。

2. 听中的活动设计(While-listening)

听力过程中设计的教学活动必须符合学生的认知水平,教师必须把握好听力活动的难度,使其呈阶梯式递进,形成有效的听力任务链,让学生能听懂。

听力材料中常有大量的信息需要在短时间内记忆,教师要培养学生边听边记的习惯与能力,以便快速捕捉相关信息,把握主题,进行判断推理。

一些学生听不懂听力内容,教师在听的过程中设计任务引导学生模仿录音中的语音语调边听边读、听中练读,从而培养听的能力,提高听课效果。教

师还可根据需要将听力材料显示在多媒体屏幕上，做适当的讲解等。

3. 听后的活动设计（After-listening）

听后活动旨在将听力材料的主题进行联系生活实际的延伸，在这一过程中，教师要深入分析和挖掘听力材料中蕴涵的信息和意义，设计考查学生听、说、读、写的延伸任务。

Integrated skills 的教学虽然没有固定的模式，但有其内在的规律。教师只有树立以学生为主体的思想，精心设计教学的各个环节，充分调动学生参与活动的积极性，才能帮助学生形成听、说、读、写的综合技能。

（二）Integrated skills 教学设计案例分析

七上　Unit 2　Let's play sports!

Integrated skills

Background

It's meaningful for the young students to do some sports after school. Students will be happy to have more activities after school.

Key words: sports, activities after school

I　Background information

Nowadays, many students are interested in playing sports. However, they have less time to do some sports after school than before because of the heavy school work. So it's important to encourage the students to go outside and enjoy themselves or have some hobbies. In this way, they can do a better job in study.

In this class, students can also know about others' favourite sports and some other hobbies through communication.

Ⅱ　Type lesson

Integrated skills training

Ⅲ　Teaching aims

By the end of the lesson, students should be able to:

1. Get the information from the listening materials.
2. Understand the main idea of the listening materials.
3. Use the information to complete the article.
4. Talk about their after-school activities.

5. Enjoy playing sports.

Ⅳ Teaching content

1. New words and phrases

2. Practice listening and speaking skills

Ⅴ Focus of the lesson and predicted area of difficulty

1. Expressions about sports

2. Help the students to get the main idea and details of the listening material about the topic

3. Lead the students to talk more about their favourite activities after school with what they've learnt

Ⅵ Teaching aids

Blackboard & Multimedia

Ⅶ Teaching procedures

Step 1 *Warm-up and lead-in (about 5 mins.)*

1. Look at the pictures and guess:

What sport do they like? What sport do they love? What sport do they enjoy?

What's their favourite sport?

2. Talk about the players:

What is Yao Ming good at?

What does Sun Yang do well in?

What sport does Sun Jike like best?

【设计理念：1. 通过看图片猜运动项目，激发兴趣的同时帮助学生复习描述喜欢的运动项目的多种句式。2. 通过谈论明星运动员所擅长的运动，进一步复习表达擅长的句式和与运动相关的表达，使学生为听说训练做好语言和心理上的准备，帮助学生热身。】

Step 2 *Before listening (about 1 min.)*

Listening tips:

(1) Read the questions quickly before listening, and pay attention to the key words.

(2) Predict while reading the questions.

(3) Listen to check the prediction.

【设计理念：通过听力的小提示这个小环节，指导学生有效听取相关信息，使学生逐渐学会听力的小技巧。听力训练是一项长期的工作，如果坚持对学生的听力学习进行有针对性的指导，学生会不断增强听力中捕捉关键信息的能力。】

Step 3 *While-listening* (*about 3 mins.*)

Listen to the tape carefully and take some notes while listening.

Step 4 *After-listening* (*about 15 mins.*)

(1) Check the answers after listening and finish the passage with what students have heard.

(2) Read the passage together.

(3) Activity: Let's make a survey. You can ask your group mates about their favourite sports. After that, please make a report to the whole class.

【设计理念：听力过程中提醒学生记录必要的信息。通过完成听后练习，以及开展进一步的围绕听力材料的小调查，使学生有效提取听力的内容，充分运用听力材料中的语言素材，并积累相关表达。】

Step 5 *Speaking* (*about 15 mins.*)

(1) Free talk

Do you like sports? Where do you often play ... ? When do you usually play ... ? Whom do you ... with? What do you often do after school?

(2) T: Sports are good for us. They are fun.

What else can we do after school? (I like music best. I like listening to music in my free time. What about you?)

Students talk about their favourite activities after school and give some reasons. They exchange ideas with each other.

【设计理念：师生对话，谈论学生喜爱的运动以及课外活动，用学生熟悉的话题激发学生思考，激活学生与话题相关的语言，在轻松快乐的氛围下进行说的训练。】

(3) Listen to the conversation and answer the question:

What activities does Sandy like to do after school?

(4) Judge the following sentences "T" or "F" and correct the mistakes:

① Music makes Sandy feel great.

② Sandy also likes playing volleyball.

③ Millie likes listening to music.

④ Millie plays volleyball with friends.

⑤ Millie reads a lot of interesting books.

(5) Read the conversation after the tape.

(6) Learn some useful expressions in the dialogue together.

What do you often do after school?

What else do you like to do/doing?

It makes me feel great. feel + *adj.* make sb. do sth.

I read a lot of interesting books. Reading is fun.

(7) Make up a new dialogue with your partner.

A: Hi, … ! What do you often do after school?

B: I often …

A: What else do you like to do?

B: I … It makes me feel great. What about you, … ?

A: I often … with my friends, and …

B: … is fun.

The teacher makes an example with a student for the rest of the students. Thus, all the students are more familiar with the dialogue.

【设计理念:通过师生对话、生生对话,从喜欢的运动扩大到经常参与的课外活动,丰富学生的话题内容;通过听并回答问题、判断正误,使学生充分了解听力中的基本信息和细节信息;通过编新对话,使学生基于生活实践学以致用。】

Step 6 *Practicing (about 5 mins.)*

Can we make our after-school activities more colorful? If so, what after-school activities are you going to do this weekend in a group? You can do some sports or just go out to have fun. What's your plan?

Students can discuss and share their different ideas with us.

(设计意图:通过小组讨论的形式,启发学生思考如何让我们的课外活动更丰富,使学生不断向往有趣、活泼的课外活动形式,无论是体育运动还是出游,同时增强学生之间的交流和分享。)

Step 7 *Homework*

(1) Remember the new words and phrases.

(2) Make a report about their friend's favourite sport.

【设计理念:巩固学生这节课所学知识,并为围绕运动的写作话题做好铺垫和准备。】

Ⅷ Blackboard design

7A Unit 2 Let's play sports

Integrated skills

1) sentence	2) phrases
What do you like to do after school?	many of, a lot of =lots of
→	
What sports do you like to play after school?	make sb. *adj.*/do sth. 使某人……
What else … ?	
Reading is fun. 动名词作主语	

Ⅸ Teaching reflection

本单元体育运动是学生们非常熟悉和喜爱的话题,本节课作为本单元的第四课时,在前面课时的铺垫下,学生已经掌握了一定量与话题相关的语言,而本节课则以听说训练为课堂重点内容,进一步培养学生的语言能力,增强相关的语言积累。

本课首先从图片导入,引导学生运用已学 What's his/her favourite sport? 谈论图片内容,同时注重变换不同句式,既复习应用又有一定趣味。对于学生喜欢的体育明星,他们更有兴趣和表达的愿望,使用 What's he/she good at? 等不同句型,使学生进一步操练,为听说活动做好充分的铺垫。

听前进行听力小技巧的温馨提醒,使学生的听力练习可以有的放矢,增强听力训练的效果;听中指导学生做好必要记录,将听到的信息及时捕捉,避免漏听和出错;1 ~2 遍的听力结束后,引导学生完成听后书本习题,针对习题设计展开一个关于同伴最喜欢的运动项目的小调查,然后再进行口头汇报,锻炼学生的口头表达能力。

由运动的话题自然过渡到学生自己平时喜欢的运动项目,并与学生进行简单的对话：为什么喜欢这个运动项目？什么时候运动？在哪里、与谁一起运动？除了体育运动之外，你还喜欢哪些课外活动？激发学生的兴趣并激活学生的相关语言。接下来的对话先以听力形式进行操练，再进行新对话的指导，让学生之间通过对话交流不同的看法，扩大语言的交际使用。

本节课学生能够较好地融入课堂，谈论他们喜欢的话题，听力训练也很有效。学生自由表达的时候自信程度和语言的准确性还有待提高，这些都需要老师不断的鼓励和关注以及学生们坚持不懈的努力。

点评：

本单元的话题“体育运动”是学生们非常熟悉和喜爱的话题，本节课的话题是谈论学生们自己喜欢的各种运动及课外进行的其他喜欢的活动，鉴于此，如何在有限的45分钟内完成该单元的综合技能训练课的教学目标，课前的精心设计就显得尤为重要。这位老师利用视听法、交际法等教学方法，把听、说、读、写有机地糅合在一起，以提高学生综合运用语言的能力。在设计每个环节时，力图结合《新课标》，深刻领会教材编写意图和本课时的教学要求，从视、听、说入手，通过师生口语交流轻松导入新课。通过听力的小提示，指导学生有效听取相关信息，使学生逐渐学会听力的小技巧。利用幻灯片、图片、录音等多种媒体，通过师生对话、生生对话、听录音、跟读、学生朗读、师生讨论等形式，将学生的个别活动、结对活动、小组活动和全班活动很好地结合起来。教师的每个教学步骤都引导学生认真思考，注重学生间的相互合作，共同发展，尤其是最后通过小组讨论的形式，启发学生思考周末活动的计划及如何让课外活动更丰富，使学生不断向往有趣活泼的课外活动形式，增强学生之间的交流和分享，进而使语言学习的过程成为学生形成积极的情感态度、主动思维、大胆实践和形成自主学习能力的过程。

七下　Unit 6　Outdoor fun

Integrated skills

Background：Outdoor activities

Everyone likes outdoor activities because they are much fun.

Key words：ourdoor activities, the history of kites

I　Background information

There are a lot of outdoor activities people do. But children will be more interested in swimming, going on picnics, especially flying kites.

The students in Grade 7 still like flying kites and will be more interested in the history of kites.

Ⅱ Type of the lesson

Integrated skills training

Ⅲ Teaching aims and learning objectives

By the end of the lesson, the students will be able to:

1. Understand the meanings of the new words. Use them in proper situations.
2. Catch necessary information from the listening materials.
3. Know the history of kites well.
4. Talk about outdoor activities with the useful expressions correctly.
5. Cooperate with partners and experience the feeling of success.

Ⅳ Teaching content

1. New words
2. The history of kites
3. Different listening skills

Ⅴ Focus of the lesson and predicted area of difficulty

1. New words and the history of the kites
2. Different listening skills
3. How to lead students to talk about the different outdoor activities

Ⅵ Teaching aids

1. Four pictures of historical people 2. Blackboard 3. Chalk
4. Computer 5. Multimedia

Ⅶ Teaching procedures

Step 1 *Warm-up and lead-in*

Play a video about outdoor activities and have a free talk before class.

T: Just how I noticed some of you studied after class. I think you can go out to relax between classes. More relaxation will make you more energetic. Let's enjoy a short video. And see what is one of you doing.

Yes, he is cycling, flying a kite, swimming, playing basketball, skating, riding, jogging ... so many outdoor activities. Then among these outdoor activities which one do you like best? And why?（找三到四个同学回答）

【设计理念：1. 导入户外活动话题。2. 用师生对话活跃课堂气氛，调动学生参与积极性。】

Step 2 *Think*

Listen and answer.

T: Everyone has his own favourite outdoor activities. Can you guess what is my favourite? ... Yes, you are so clever. I like flying kites for fun. But when I go out for fun, I don't know what I can do and I can't do and what I should take. Our old friend Amy and her cousin Shirley are going out for a picnic. And let's listen and fill in the table.

A day out	
Feelings	
What they can do	
What the can't do	
Things they should take	

【设计理念：1. 操练导入部分的活动。2. 训练学生听的能力。】

Step 3 *Discuss*

T: In this conversation, Amy tells us what to do and what not to do for a picnic. But there are many more things we need to think about and pay attention to in our lives. Please think about: What can you do? What can't you do ? And why? What can you take? Now work in groups and write down the list. Try to write down as many as you can.

OK, let's check.

First, what can we do? We can fly kites, go jogging and enjoy the view ...

Second, what can't we do? We can't climb the trees, swim in the river, walk on the grass, throw rubbish(垃圾) ...

Last, what can we take? Food, drinks, mattress, umbrella ...

【设计理念：1. 锻炼学生思考问题的能力。2. 培养学生合作解决问题的能力。】

Step 4 *Present* (*Pair work*)

Go out for a picnic

T: Tomorrow is Saturday. And it will be very sunny.

A: We are having a picnic today. I'm so ... Maybe it's a good time for you to have a picnic. Now talk with your partner about it. (找三组同学回答)

B: Me too. It'll be a great day.

A: What can we do there?

B: We can ...

A: Good. Can we ... too?

B: No, I'm afraid not. It's dangerous/ ... to ... Yes, Of course. It's exciting/ ... to ...

A: I see.

Remember to take/bring ...

B: OK ...

【设计理念：1. 锻炼学生说的能力。2. 鼓励学生应用刚刚所用的知识。】

Step 5 *Lead-in*

T: Some students like flying kites, but do you know something about kites?

T: If you don't, it does not matter. One of my friends in Weifang, Shangdong Province told me something about kites. Now let's listen to the material and try to answer the two questions:

When did people in Weifang begin to make kites?

When was the first International Kites Festival held in Weifang?

T: People in Weifang designed their own beautiful kites. If you design your own kite, what will it look like?

T: I also design many beautiful kites. Look at them. Tell me what it looks like.

T: You are so great. Some other students also design their own kites. What do they look like? Look at Part A1. Listen to the conversation and write down the students' names under their kites.

【设计理念：通过自制听力内容增加学生对潍坊风筝节的了解从而对处理之后的听力部分做好铺垫。】

Step 6 *Think*

T: Flying kites is interesting and many people like it. But how much do you know about the history of kites?

Look at the five questions:

Q1: Which country were kites born?

Q2: Who made the first kite in China?

Q3: What did the first kite look like?

Q4: What did people use to make the first kite?

Q5: How did kites become famous all over the world?

T: It does not matter. I would like to introduce another four people to you, and then you will learn better about it.

Now let us play a guessing game. I will show you some pictures or some words. Can you tell me who the person is? Here are the rules: The first one to give us the correct answer, your group will get one star. Let us see which group will be the winner.

T: You are so clever. We know the four people are closely related but do you know what did they do to help kites become famous all over the world?

T: It does not matter. Now let us listen to the material and finish Part A2: Write the correct letters in the boxes.

T: They helped a lot to make Chinese kites famous. But when did the Chinese people begin to make kites? Now let us listen again and fill in the blanks with correct words.

【设计理念：以一个猜的游戏介绍四位历史人物及其对风筝产生和推广做出的贡献来增加学生对风筝历史的了解，并且为下面的听力部分做好铺垫。】

Step 7 *Discuss and retell the history of kites*

T: After learning so much about the history of kites, how much do you remember it? Now close your books. Works in groups and try to retell the history of kites from three aspects: when/who or what place/what happened.

discuss **Review the history of kites!**

When	Who/What place	What happened
in the Warring States period	Mo Zi ...	...
...	...	...
...	...	...
...	...	...

【设计理念:以复述听力内容和填充表格的方式来帮助学生复习、巩固上述听力材料文本,加强学生对风筝历史的掌握。】

Step 8 *Group work*

T: The next International Kites Festival in Weifang is coming. Many foreigners will come to see it. Your group will be invited(被邀请) to give a talk about Chinese kites. It includes:

* history of kites (4 periods)
* beautiful kites(material, shape ...)
* your hope

You can report like this: Good morning, ladies and gentlemen:

Welcome to Weifang, China. We are very glad to give you a talk about Chinese kites here.

First, we'd like to introduce the history of Chinese kites ...

Then we will show you some beautiful kites.

We use ... to make kites. They have different shapes. Some look like ... Some look like ... You are sure to like them.

At last, we hope ...

【设计理念:通过要求学生小组合作,准备一个关于中国风筝的讲座来操练以上所学内容并且在合作的过程中培养合作精神。】

Step 9 *Summarize*

T: Today we learn that kites are also an important part of Chinese culture. When we have free time, do not always watch TV or play computer games. You had better go out to do something such as flying kites and go near the nature.

【设计理念：老师简明扼要地总结本堂课所学内容，并且进行主题升华：让中国的风筝文化走向世界。】

Ⅷ Blackboard design

Words: wood period century
excited mobile phone

Phrases: make a bird out of wood
use bamboo to make kites
in the 13th century
from then on
become famous for

Sentence structures:
It is dangerous to do ...
Remember to take your mobile phone.
Now everything is ready.
Shall we go?

Group	Score
1	
2	
3	
4	
5	
6	

Ⅸ Teaching reflection

本节课以6个微视频来导入课外活动,既提供了相关的背景知识,又激发了学生的学习兴趣,然后通过师生对话活跃课堂气氛,调动学生参与积极性,再通过小组间的讨论,锻炼学生用英语思维的能力,同时培养学生合作解决问题的能力。之后以自制听力来介绍中国潍坊的风筝,为学生提供背景信息,从而为下面的听力内容的处理做好了铺垫。再以一个猜的游戏介绍四位历史人物及其对风筝产生和推广做出的贡献来增加学生对风筝历史的了解。并通过填表格练习帮助学生梳理听力内容,为复述做好准备,但听完立刻让学生复述还是有难度的,可以进行一个过渡环节,例如,安排一个小组对话,让学生对文本较为熟悉之后再复述。

点评:

在本节课的教学中,老师能通过 Discuss(Step 3)部分的开展,不仅锻炼学生思考问题的能力和培养学生合作解决问题的能力,还通过讨论,渗透德育,如 We can't walk on the grass/climb the trees/throw rubbish;还对学生进行了安全教育,如 We can't swim in the river 等。在 Pair work(Step 4)中,设计周末去野餐的情境，锻炼学生说的能力，鼓励学生及时应用所学的知识，教师还通过自制听力内容（Step 5），增加学生对潍坊风筝节的了解，既扩大了学生的知识面，也为接下来的听力部分做好了铺垫。但是在 Step 2 和 Step 3 之间，可以让学生读一读 Speak up 的对话，确保学生能顺利完成 Step 4 中 pair work 的任务。

八上 Unit 4 Do it yourself
Integrated skills

Background

Everyone is interested in DIY because it is very new and can make people creative.

Key words: do it yourself, make a fruit salad

Ⅰ Background information

DIY stands for doing it yourself and is very attractive to students. The students in Grade 8 still like DIY and will be more interested in DIY.

Ⅱ Type of the lesson

Integrated skills training

Ⅲ Teaching aims and learning objectives

By the end of the lesson, the students will be able to:

1. Understand the meanings of the new words. Use them in proper situations.
2. Catch necessary information from the listening materials.
3. Know something of how to make a fruit salad.
4. Talk about making a fruit salad with the useful expressions correctly.
5. Cooperate with partners and experience the feeling of success.

Ⅳ Teaching content

1. New words
2. How to make a fruit salad
3. Different listening skills

Ⅴ Focus of the lesson and predicted area of difficulty

1. New words and how to make a fruit salad
2. Different listening skills

3. How to lead students to talk about making a fruit salad

Ⅵ Teaching aids

1. Four pictures of historical people　2. Blackboard　3. Chalk
4. Computer　5. Multimedia

Ⅶ Teaching procedures

Step 1 *Warm-up and lead-in*

Play a video about outdoor activities and free talk before class.

T：First，let's enjoy a video. What is it about?

S：A fruit salad.

T：Do you know how to make a fruit salad?（板书，带读）

S：Choose fruit.

T：You should choose fruit in season.（板书，带读）Because they are very fresh. I think you shouldn't choose these. Because they are not in season. They are：

S：purple　grapes　strawberries（板书，带读）

T：Then what should we do?

S：Wash the fruit.

T：Do you need any tools if you want to cut them?

S：knife　fork　plate　bowl

T：Maybe you also need some spoons.（板书，带读）You can use the tools to cut some of the larger fruit into small pieces. Finally，what should we do?

S：Mix them together.

T：And you can also add some salad cream if you like. Do you want to give any tips when making a fruit salad?

S：Use fruit of different colors，and try to make your fruit salad look as good as it tastes. Don't leave it in the air for some time because some of the fruit will turn brown.

【设计理念：通过视频导入今天上课的水果沙拉话题。吸引学生的注意力和关注度。从课堂一开始就紧紧地调动学生的积极性。同时用师生对话活跃课堂气氛，调动学生参与积极性。】

Step 2 *Think*

Listen and answer.

T：Andy and Suzy are making a fruit salad. Listen to their conversation and tick the things they need.

a watermelon	grapes	strawberry
a bowl	a spoon	apples
salad cream	plates	bananas

T：Read Amy's notes of how to make a fruit salad. Put her notes in the correct order. Write the numbers 1–4 in the boxes.

A2：

Wash the fruit.

Mix them together. Add some salad cream if you like.

Cut some of the larger fruit into small pieces.

Choose your favourite fruit.

T：Now listen to the tips that Suzy gives Amy for making a fruit salad. Help Amy complete her notes with the correct words.

A3：Tips for making a fruit salad

Choose your favourite fruit. Use fruit ________. Make sure it is ________.

Use fruit of ________ colors and try to make your fruit salad look ________ it tastes. For example, mixing red apples, green ________, purple grapes and ________ together will make the salad look very colourful.

Prepare the fruit salad ________ you are going to eat it. Some of the fruit will quickly ________ when you leave it ________ for some time.

【设计理念：前面的导入过程中已经给学生的听力做好了铺垫，因此学生只需要在听的过程中抓住关键词，完成听力练习。学生在预习的基础上完成听力练习并训练学生的听力。】

Step 3 *Lead in and listen to fill*

T：Maybe some of you like making fruit salads. But I would like to make sandwiches. What do we need?

S：Vegetables, bread.

T：We also need some ham.（板书，带读）They are quick and easy to make. Sometimes, you need tomato source.（板书，带读）

T：Sandy and her mum are talking about what to eat for lunch. Listen and fill the blanks.

How to make sandwich

Pick a piece of bread

Put some tomato sauce on it

Put some ham and vegetables on it

Put another piece of bread on the top of it

【设计理念：1. 在导入完水果沙拉的基础上，导入下一个要讨论的话题，学生更容易接受并且吸收。2. 培养学生独立思考的能力，培养学生自己动手做食物的兴趣，提高课堂的趣味性。】

Step 4 *Present*（*Pair work*）

Go out for a picnic

T：Now talk about what you really want to know.

A：It's time for ... Can we stop ... ?

B：OK. Let's make ...

A：So we had better prepare ...

B：Right. First, ... What's next?

A：Next, we can ...

B：That's correct. Then ... Finished.

【设计理念：1. 在前面的讨论环节学生已经列举了跟三明治食物有关的词汇，pair work 要求学生两两合作，编一个新的对话，能锻炼学生说的能力和口语表达的能力。2. 鼓励学生能够活学活用，将其他同学想到的活动编进自己的对话中。】

Step 5 *Lead-in*

T：I am crazy about ice cream. So I want to share with you how to make mango ice cream.

* Prepare some milk, eggs, sugar, cream and mangoes
* Cut the mangoes into pieces

* Mix the sugar and eggs. Then stir (搅拌) them until it turns white
* Cook the milk
* Add milk to the eggs and milk
* Add mangoes to them
* Put it into the fridge

Tips:

* Don't cook the milk for a long time, but just for some time.
* You had better add chocolate or fruit to make it taste better and look better.
* Don't put it into the fridge when it's still hot.

【设计理念：在简单的水果名称和三明治的基础之上，增加学生对水果沙拉的了解以及怎样制作水果沙拉，从而为下面的小组活动做好铺垫。让学生在英语课堂学到更多的生活常识。】

Step 6 *Group work*

T: You're going to have a picnic with your best friends in Bochishan Park. Please discuss in groups. Make sure your food looks as good as it tastes. Your report should include:

* What to make
* What you need
* How to make it
* Tips
* What's special about it

【设计理念：学生通过本节课的学习可以掌握关于 DIY 水果沙拉和三明治的英文表达方法，从而尝试写出自己的 DIY 水果沙拉的故事。这个活动旨在帮助学生练习巩固本节课所学的 DIY 的英文表达方法。】

Step 7 *Summarize*

T: Today we learn how to make a fruit salad. When we have time, do not always watch TV and play computer games, you had better go out to do something such as doing DIY works.

【设计理念：总结本堂课所学内容，并且进行主题升华。让学生在课外

之余尝试自己亲自动手做些自己喜欢的 DIY 作品。鼓励学生不要天天待在家中玩电脑,享受动手的乐趣。】

Step 6 *Homework*

Make something for your parents and then write the process(过程)down.

Ⅷ Blackboard design

grape mix　　example　　leave

strawberry　　salad

Group	Score
1	
2	
3	
4	
5	
6	

Ⅸ Teaching reflection

通过视频导入本节课话题,直截了当,也很快吸引了学生的注意力。老师对学生的照顾太多,对学生不太放心。老师不断降低难度,让学生能够完成任务,能够听得懂,能够完成对话。但是这个度要把握好,比如前面导入的香蕉和葡萄,有些单词可能学生小学就已经会了,但是老师还是再导入一遍。出发点很好,尤其是面对基础不好的学生,降低难度,培养自信心,培养对英语学习的兴趣。但前面做的铺垫太多,在每次听听力前都有导入,这样就有点浪费时间。有的单词不需要导入,不需要做太多的铺垫。给学生一个机会,让他自己说出这个词,激发学生课外提前拓展更多的英语知识。如果学生没有机会去思考,去展示自己,那样英语课的课外拓展基本上就是零。铺垫到何处,值得思考。可以在教学的过程中去教授学生。老师要放手学生,给他们多一点自信心。

点评:

在本节课的教学中,老师能从学生的生活实际出发,引起学生对所听内容产生兴趣;为了降低听力难度,提高听的效果,老师在听前设计了一些活动,进行生词的感知和短语的梳理。通过课堂教学的各个环节,帮助学生培养听、说、读、写的综合技能。

在 Step 1 Warm-up and lead-in 环节中,教师直接用 First, let's enjoy a

video. 导入本课的学习。其实,在放视频前,也可和学生进行简短的 free talk。比如,Do you make food for yourself every day? Can you make this kind of food? Let's watch a video. 通过谈学生自己的生活,迅速拉近师生的距离。

要让学生取得好的听的效果,就要教给学生听的方法,教给学生预测的方法尤为重要。在做 A2、A3 练习之前,可进行听力技巧的指导。引导学生对听的内容进行预测。

在学生听完对话,完成填空练习后,可以让学生读一读对话,为下一步的 pair work 做好铺垫。

group work 的出发点很好,让学生通过活动,尝试写出自己的 DIY 水果沙拉和三明治的英文表达方法。但 DIY 就是“自己动手做”,最好不要限制学生 DIY 的表达角度,可扩展 DIY 的内容,如相册、风筝、小首饰、纸艺、布艺、玩具等,让学生自主选择,最终形成 DIY 的汇报成果。甚至老师还可以帮学生准备一些简单的材料,让学生在口头汇报的同时,展示一下小组 DIY 的真正成果。达到在“学中做”,在“做中学”。

八下 Unit 7 International charities

Integrated skills

Background

There are many international charities in the world. They help the people in need in different ways. Students will develop the idea of trying to help the charities.

Key words: international charities

I Background information

There are many international charities in the world. They help the people in need in different ways. In this unit, students will know five international charities. They are UNICEF, Oxfam, World Vision, ORBIS and WWF.

In Reading, students understand the charity work in ORBIS.

II Type lesson

Integrated skills training

III Teaching aims

By the end of the lesson, students should be able to:

1. Get some information of UNICEF by different listening methods.

2. Read and recite Speak up, master some basic sentences and make up new conversations about seeing a doctor.

3. Develop the students' abilities of listening and speaking.

Ⅳ Teaching content

1. New words and phrases

2. Listening, Reading skills

3. Learn with fun

Ⅵ Focus of the lesson and predicted area of difficulty

1. New words:

war, organize(*v.*)—organization(*n.*), pale, matter, check

2. Phrases:

make the world a better place for children prevent sb. from getting illness look pale feel well get toothache have a check take the medicine in a few days be proud to do sth. keep asking myself

3. Sentences:

(1) At that time, many children's lives were changed because of the war.

(2) It is important for children to receive basic education.

(3) Take this medicine after meals three times a day.

(4) No time to be nervous any more!

To understand and respond to the factual information presented in the radio program.

Ⅵ Teaching aids

1. Video 2. Pictures 3. Blackboard 4. Chalk

5. Computer 6. Multimedia

Ⅶ Teaching procedures

Step 1 *Revision*

T: Good morning/afternoon, boys and girls. We talked international charities in this unit. Let's review some charities we learnt in this unit. I will show you the logos of them. Tell us their names and their function. The first one, which charity does it mean?

S: ...

T：What does ORBIS do?

S：…

T：What does WWF do?

S：

T：What does Oxfam do?

S：…

T：Who can help children in poor countries?

S：…

T：How much do you know about UNICEF? Please discuss with your partners.

S：…

【设计理念：在课堂开始时先呈现 Welcome 部分的四个国际慈善机构的徽标，让学生说出机构的名称及基本的工作范畴，过程中就复习了 Welcome 的 B 部分。】

Step 2 *Presentation*

T：In the world, there are many poor children need our help. Look at the picture. He is a little boy from Africa. It is short of water there. They need water very much. But who can help them?

S：…

T：How much do you know about UNICEF?

S：…

T：UNICEF is part of the United Nations and it was set up in Europe in 1946. Do you want to know more about it?

S：…

T：Look at the website. It's the UNICEF website. Let's click on the icon "about us" and we will learn more about the charity. Now read the short passage of A1 and answer the questions in A3.（调整一下书上练习的顺序，先处理 A3 部分，再处理 A2 和 A4 听力部分）

1. When was UNICEF set up?

2. Why was UNICEF set up?

3. Where does UNICEF work?

4. What does UNICEF do?

T：Please underline the red parts.

be part of … be set up … because of … make the world a better place for children（Read together）

T：Daniel is listening to a radio programme about UNICEF. Help him put the sentences in the correct order. First, read the five sentences. Can you judge the first and the last sentences?（跟学生强调听听力前一定要先读题，画出重点部分，并去预测听力的答案）

S：…

T：It's very easy, but it's difficult for us to judge the number of the rest three sentences. So, listen to the tape carefully and write the numbers 1–5 in the boxes.（听听力时要整体把握文章大意，根据题目有针对性地听细节）

S：（Do A2）

T：Daniel is writing the report on UNICEF. Complete his report with the information on Page 101. Then listen to Daniel and check your answers.（先让学生根据A1、A2、A3部分的信息填写A4，尽可能填写，填写不出来的，听听力时有针对性地听）

S：（Do A4, check and read together.）

T：Please translate the following language points.

1. 那时，由于战争，许多孩子的生活都被改变了。
2. 为孩子们将世界变成一个更美好的地方。
3. 接受基础教育对于孩子们来说很重要。
4. 通过……筹集资金
5. 组织其他的活动
6. 作为志愿者工作

【设计理念：先呈现几张图片，引出问题：谁能帮助这些贫困地区的儿童？一来激发学生的学习兴趣，二来引入本节课讨论的主题，三让学生能够对比进而珍惜自己现有的生活。接着呈现UNICEF的网站，很真实的情境，学生也乐于去接受下面的教学任务：阅读A1部分回答A3相关问题，培养学生的阅读、寻找细节的能力。过程中老师要呈现一些重要的短语，如：because of, make the world a better place for children, set up等。接着创设情境：Daniel

要学习了解 UNICEF 的相关信息并要完成一份报告，让学生通过听力来寻找信息，培养听力能力。老师要教会学生听力的技巧：学会预测、整体把握、寻找细节。过程中呈现重要的短语：work as a volunteer, provide sth. for sb./provide sb. with sth. 等。最后再通过一些翻译句子来巩固所学内容。】

Step 3 *Speak up*

T：UNICEF tries to prevent children from getting illnesses. When you look pale, you'd better see a doctor. The doctor will give you a check to find out what is the matter with you. Look at the picture. What's the matter with him?

S：...（He's got toothache.）（老师带读短语）

T：The boy goes to a health centre of UNICEF. He is talking to the doctor. Let's listen to the tape and answer some questions.

1. How long has the boy felt bad?

2. Will the boy be all right in a few days?

T：After listening and answering, maybe you know some details. Here are some sentences. Are they true or false?

1. The boy does not look very well.

2. His face is red.

3. He has felt like this for three days.

4. He will be all right in a few days.

5. He has to take the medicine four times a day.

T：Let's read after the tape and underline the red parts by yourself.（圈画出一些就医的基本用语、重要短语和句型）

T：Work in pairs and make up a new conversation about seeing a doctor.（掌握就医的基本用语，能展开相关谈话）

（Pair work）

【设计理念：由 UNICEF 的工作过渡到日常的看病就医中，让学生掌握就医的基本步骤，并能自己编写新的对话，鼓励学生创新。】

Step 4 *Practice*

T：Finish the following exercises.

1. UNICEF wants children to be ________（health）.

2. UNICEF makes the world a(n) ________ (good) place for children.

3. It provides ________ (educate) for poor children.

4. The organization raises money by ________ (organize) activities.

5. Many children's ________ (life) were changed because of the war.

6. 你看起来很苍白，请饭前服药。

7. 我爸爸几天后将会回来。

【设计理念：做一些题目来复习巩固今天所讲的一些重要的知识点。】

Step 5 *Group work*

T: We know many people and animals need our help. What or who do you think needs our help most? Which charity can help them? What can we do to help them? Discuss in groups.（展示一些濒临灭绝的动物和需要帮助的人，给学生一些启发。小组选择一项开始讨论并形成一篇报道来呈现）

S: (Discuss in groups and choose two or three groups to present their reports.)

T: We live in the same world but have quite different life. We should cherish our life and try our best to help the people in need. Let's make the world a better place for everyone together!

【设计理念：在前面 Welcome，Reading 及本节课的大量输入之后，让学生选择最需要帮助的人或动物、哪些慈善机构能够帮助他们，并讨论我们可以怎样来支持慈善机构的工作。锻炼学生的语言组织和运用能力，并通过这个活动激发学生的爱心和互助心。】

Step 6 *Homework*

(1) Complete the worksheet.

(2) Preview task. Write a short passage about UNICEF.

【设计理念：复习巩固本节课所学并能在日常生活中运用；先写一篇关于 UNICEF 的作文，为下个课时的学习做好准备。】

Ⅷ Blackboard design

8B Unit 7 Integrated skills

war pale	work as a volunteer
matter check	What's the matter?

organize　　　　　　　　Well, it's nothing serious.

Ⅸ　Teaching reflection

这节课从复习 Welcome 部分的国际慈善机构及其职能开始,接着导入到本课时的内容: UNICEF 及其职能。通过阅读 A1 让学生获悉具体细节信息并完成书上的 A3 部分。在听力练习之前要进行听力指导: 阅读题目、画出重点短语或单词、预测答案。学生在平时的训练中已经养成了良好的听力习惯。接着完成 A4,先根据前三个部分完成部分空格,填不出的在听的过程中要重点听、抓关键词。我们在平时的教学中一定要注重学法和做题方法的指导,例如听力,要跟学生强调: 掌握大意、抓住重点。

Speak up 部分要学生掌握一些就医的基本术语,并能根据范文自己编对话,老师要尽可能地让更多的学生站起来呈现自己的对话,并且要求其他的同学学会倾听、改错,老师要肯定站起来的同学并鼓励更多的学生参与到课堂中。

最后的大活动是学生选择自己觉得最需要帮助的人或物、哪个慈善机构可以帮助他们、做些什么去帮助他们。在活动的过程中,学生运用所学组织语言,同时也在教育他们: 要珍惜自己的生活,帮助需要帮助的人,让地球变成我们共同的美好的家园。

点评:

在本节课的教学中,老师通过学生熟悉的四个国际慈善机构的徽标,引导学生复习前面学过的慈善机构的名称及基本的工作范畴,既激发学生的学习兴趣,又很好地引入了本节课讨论的主题;在新知呈现的过程中,教师能适宜地调整一下书上练习的顺序,先处理 A1、A3 部分,再处理 A2 和 A4 听力部分。首先,通过阅读 A1 部分回答 A3 部分的相关问题(问题 1—问题 4),培养学生的阅读和寻找细节的能力。过程中老师呈现了一些重要的短语,接着创设情境,让学生通过听力来寻找信息,培养听的能力,并从学会预测、整体把握、寻找细节等方面对学生进行听力技巧的指导。过程中呈现重要短语并通过一些练习来巩固所学内容。课堂教学的各个环节环环相扣,体现了教师的教学设计能力。通过课堂教学的各个环节的开展,积极有效地帮助学生培养听、说、读、写的综合技能。在 Speak up 教学中,老师在学生掌握就医基本术语的基础上,鼓励学生自己编写新的对话,鼓励学生创新。最后的 group work,让学生自主选择最需要帮助的人或动物,分析哪些慈善机构能够帮助他们,并讨论我们可以怎样来支持慈善机构的工作。不仅锻炼了学生的语言组织和运用能力,而且通过这个活动激发学生的爱心和互助心,渗透德育意识。

九上 Unit 2 Colours

Integrated skills

Background

The color therapy can help us change our moods according to the colors we prefer.

Key words: color therapy, different clothes, occasions

Ⅰ Background information

According to the theory of color therapy, we can choose the colors we like to influence our moods. When we absorb the power brought by the colors, it will go to the place where it is needed inside our body. In this way, different parts of our body will be in harmony.

Ⅱ Type of the lesson

Integrated skills training

Ⅲ Teaching aims and learning objectives

By the end of the lesson, the students will be able to:

1. Understand the meanings of the new words.
   Use them in proper situations.
2. Gain useful information from the given listening materials.
3. Ask for advice and also give advice on colors.
4. State the merits and demerits of different clothes and the function of colors.
5. Cooperate with partners and experience the feeling of success.

Ⅳ Teaching content

1. New words and phrases
2. Listening skills
3. Speaking skills

Ⅴ Focus of the lesson and predicted area of difficulty

1. New words and phrases

2. Listening and speaking skills

3. How to give advice on colors

Ⅵ Teaching aids

1. Blackboard 2. Chalk 3. Computer 4. Multimedia

5. Projector

Ⅶ Teaching procedures

Step 1 *Free talk and lead-in*

(1) Show some pictures about the food therapy to lead in the topic.

T: Boys and girls, autumn is coming. It's time for us to keep healthy. Look at the picture. What is it about? It's about food therapy. (带读) Do you think food can influence our health? Different kinds of food have a different influence on our health. I prefer(板书) green vegetables. That is to say, I would rather eat (板书,带读) green vegetables. I would rather not(板书,反复操练) eat snacks. What about you? So food influences us deeply. What about colors? Can they influence us? How? Millie has found an advertisement for the color therapy. Let's find out the power of the color therapy.

【设计理念:通过用生活中的食疗自然引入颜色疗法,更贴近真实语境,使学生能够有话可说。本节有 would rather do 的重要句式,通过导入与谈论食疗操练有关的句式,加深学生对重点句型的把握。】

(2) Read the advertisement and answer questions.

T: Read the advertisement for Mrs Rainbow's color therapy and answer the following questions.

① How can the color therapy help us?

② How much do we have to pay for the color therapy?

③ What if the color therapy doesn't work?

④ Where is Mrs Rainbow's color therapy centre?

⑤ What channel will the programme *The Teens Show* be on?

T: Now let's check the answers.

【设计理念:学生通过阅读广告,简单地了解有关 Mrs Rainbow 的色彩疗法的基本信息,先填写①②③空格,然后阅读接下来的信息,根据现实生活的经验,猜测可能的对话内容,提高听力理解的准确性。】

Step 2 *Listening practice and pair work*

(1) Play the tape and ask students to listen to the interview with Mrs Rainbow and help Millie complete her notes in Part A1.

T: After reading the advertisement above, you have already known something about the color therapy. There is an interview with Mrs Rainbow. Listen carefully and try to fill in the blanks with the exact answers you hear from the interview. (教师在教室巡视,发现学生听力盲点)

T: The listening material is not very difficult. Let's check the answers.

【设计理念:通过听录音材料,进一步了解颜色疗法。】

(2) Ask students to listen to Suzy's questions and help Millie answer them.

T: Suzy wants to learn something about Mrs Rainbow. Listen to her questions and help Millie answer them. Pretend you are Millie. Circle the correct letters.

T: When you listen to the tape, please pay special attention to the six questions Suzy has asked. Then choose the correct answers in Part A3.

T: Let's check the answers.

【设计理念:学生在完成 Part 1 后,已经了解了颜色疗法。在回答 Suzy 的问题时,能够检测学生对前一部分听力材料的理解情况,并得到丰富的输入材料,为接下来的口语表达打下基础。】

(3) Pair work—Students work together with their partners and make up a dialogue.

T: Suppose you want to ask Mrs Rainbow for help about colors. Before you go there, you want to know something about the color therapy. Make up a dialogue between you and Mrs Rainbow. Ask at least five questions.

T: First let me give you an example. Hello, Mrs Rainbow. Can I ask you a few questions about your color therapy? Where can I find you? How much does it cost? What can I do if I don't feel confident enough? Recently I feel a bit stressed. What should I do? Which color can cheer me up? Thank you very much! See you soon.

T: Now, go ahead.

【设计理念:两人一组编对话,创设真实的情境,让学生角色扮演讨论颜色疗法,能够让学生运用所学的知识实现交流的目的。前面两次听力练习已经为学生提供一定的语言输入,学生已经可以用英语介绍颜色疗法。教师充分创造机会,使学生能对课本进行巩固并充分锻炼口语,提高语言表达技能。】

Step 3 *Speak up*

What color do you prefer?

T: The color therapy tells us that colors can influence our moods. When people are in different colors, they are in different moods. What color do you prefer? (操练 prefer, would rather 句型) Why?

【设计理念:根据 Speak up 对话中的内容,设计问题让学生熟悉话题。让学生谈论自己喜欢的颜色,贴近生活,增加语言教学的真实性。注重学生口语能力的锻炼和提高,充分创造机会让学生开口说英语。】

Students listen to the tape and answer questions.

T: Different people like different colors. Andy and Millie are also talking about what color to wear to a party. Let's find out what colors they prefer.

① Does Andy like red?

② What color does he like?

③ Which trousers does he prefer to wear? Why?

T: Let's check the answers.

【设计理念:先让学生浏览问题,带着问题听录音,让学生在听力理解时有一定的导向性,提高理解的准确性。】

(3) Pair work—Students make up a dialogue with their partners.

T: When you grow up, you all have to work. But before that, you will have a job interview. What should you wear? How to make yourself remembered among all the job applicants? Ask your partners for advice.

T: Let me set an example for you. Hi, Millie. I'm going to a job interview. But I don't know what to wear. Can you tell whether these clothes look good on me? I think the blouse looks good on me. But which color should I wear? White or blue? Blue can calm me down. It's a good choice. What about trousers? Black? Yes. Black matches my blue blouse very well. Thank you very much! I feel more confident now.

【设计理念:在课本对话中给出的情境是参加生日派对。但在日常生活中我们会遇到各种各样的情境,而工作面试是几乎每个人都要经历的。通过设计这个情境,帮助学生扩大语言交际范围,在多种情境中锻炼口语表达能力。】

Step 4 *Group work*

T: In our daily life, we can change our moods by wearing different kinds of colors. Can you think of any other ways to change your moods? Discuss in groups.

T: Some of you say listening to music is a good way to relax if you are stressed. Some say reading a book can also calm you down. Talking to parents or friends can help us a lot. You are all right. You've done a very good job. There are many other ways to change our moods. Now we are in Grade Nine. Many of us feel stressed. Remember not to keep your problems to yourselves.

【设计理念:本节课主要讨论颜色疗法即颜色的作用。但在日常生活中,还有不同的途径可以调节我们的心情,话题源自于课本,但又高于课本,达到了新的升华。学生发散思维,进行自主讨论,以小组合作的方式,在合作中学习。】

Step 5 *Conclusion and proverbs*

T: Colors can help us keep calm. They can also make us creative. They are really powerful. If we have problems, try to use colors to help yourselves. If colors can not help solve your problems, you can still go to your teachers or parents or think of other ways because life is not a single line, a road leading nowhere, you can turn. You can always find ways to solve your problems.

【设计理念:升华主题,启发学生,遇到问题,解决问题,生活没有过不去的坎。学会调节自己的心情,找出方法,解决问题。勇敢积极地面对人生。】

Step 6 *Homework*

(1) Recite words and phrases.

(2) Surf the Internet and find another kind of therapy and write a report on it.

(3) Preview task.

【设计理念:通过这样的作业争取让每一个孩子将当堂所学知识加以应用。学生查找信息,扩大知识面。鼓励学生积极主动学习,用所学句型介绍

新的疗法,巩固所学内容。】

Ⅷ Blackboard design

9A Unit 2 Colors—Integrated skills

practice	would rather do than do
discover	prefer doing to doing
promise	suggest doing
work	suggest sth. to sb.

Ⅸ Teaching reflection

本节课话题主要围绕色彩展开,由于听力部分材料是关于色彩疗法的,学生比较生疏,因此在导入时就以食疗的话题开始,贴近学生生活,让学生有话可说。教学流程充分考虑学生的能力,从学生熟悉的话题到新知,从课本材料输入到学生语言输出,各个环节层层递进。课堂各项环节的设计都是基于小组合作的形式,运用了 pair work, group work 等活动,将课本内容和课外拓展进行有效的结合,增强学生的综合语言运用能力,体现以学生为主体的课堂教学理念。

在两两对话环节,有部分基础较弱的同学在访问时无话可说,不能准确地组织语言。在两两对话讨论搭配衣服参加工作面试时,学生较难表达出准确的句子,缺乏必要的生活经验基础,教师应给予适当的导入扩充或通过图片展示等方式,补充学生的知识缺失,为对话做好充分的基础准备。

点评:

本课时教师利用现有教材,通过教学过程中的听前、听中和听后的活动,从学生熟悉的话题到新知,从课本材料输入到学生语言输出,各个环节层层递进,培养学生听、说、读、写的综合技能。

导入部分,教师通过用生活中的食疗自然引入颜色疗法,更贴近真实语境,使学生能够有话可说。并在情境中引出本节课的重要句式 would rather do,加深学生对重点句型的把握。

通过阅读广告内容,先让学生填写 A1 部分的(1)(2)(3)空格,然后根据现实生活经验,引导学生猜测采访 Mrs Rainbow 可能的对话内容,这种对听的内容进行的预测,建立在学生个人知识、经验和推理等基础之上,有利于学生取得更好的听的结果。

在 A2、A3 听力材料完成后，教师创设真实的情境，让学生角色扮演讨论颜色疗法，使学生能对课本进行巩固并充分锻炼口语，提高语言表达技能。同时达成让学生运用所学的知识实现交流的目的。

在 Speak up 部分，在听对话前，教师先让学生浏览问题，带着问题听录音，让学生在听力理解时有一定的导向性，提高了理解的准确性。

五、 Task 课型

作为一个单元的收尾,Task 课型旨在让学生在本单元已学的基础上,梳理思路,组织语言,形成篇章。在培养学生写作能力的同时,使学生对本单元已学内容达到灵活运用。

写作是综合性较强的语言运用形式,是用英语表达思想的言语活动。英语写作具有三个特点:1. 借助书写符号进行的(在同样的时间内所包含的信息量小于口语,表达速度慢于口语);2. 准备程度较高(深思熟虑,仔细推敲,反复修改);3. 要求标准较高(更加强调语言的正确性、逻辑性和严谨性)。

(一)Task 课型特点及设计要求

Task 课型的教学方法一般将情景教学和任务型教学相结合,其中更侧重于任务型教学。在教学设计时,教师应该依据本课内容,创设合适的教学情景,结合书本内容和所设情景,形成本节课的一条主线,围绕这条主线设计教学活动,将各个教学环节有机结合在一起。教学环节的设计需要教师关注呈现、操练以及反馈。针对 Task 课型,教学环节应涵盖:语言输入、文本处理、拓展铺垫和写作评价。

语言输入环节中教师根据教学情景,设计适合的教学活动,导入本课生词和短语。在本环节,教师也可以有意识地去渗透写作思路和篇章结构,同时也可以增加与写作内容相关的语言和信息输入,为学生之后写作做好铺垫。文本处理,教师引导学生阅读学习范文。在这一环节,学生需要从范文中获取写作所需要的语言表达方式,将上一环节习得的单词和短语组织成语句。学生更重要的任务是从范文中梳理写作思路,形成写作框架。拓展铺垫,是在以上教学环节的基础上,设计教学活动,让学生操练所学语言表达和写作框架。在该环节,教师要有意识地根据写作框架设计学生活动,引导学生按照这一框架去表述。此外,教师不能局限于文本,要打开学生思维,设计活动使学生有足够的空间去丰富写作需要的信息和语言表达。写作评价,作为最后一个主要环节,需要孩子动笔书写,形成篇章。在写作之前,教师应让学生知道评价一篇好作文的标准,引导学生按照这一标准去写作,更好地完成写作任务。在评价环节,也应引导学生先自评后互评,促进学生自己发现问题,取长补短,继而再由教师评价,给学生更有指导意义的点评,让学生能更好地完善作文。

以上只是对 Task 课型基本教学思路的阐释。教师在设计教学流程时,可以对每一个教学环节进行丰富,并设置可以调动学生积极性的活动。例如,增加对写作技巧的指导,增加小组讨论互评作文等环节。Task 课型要让学生在愉快的环境下锻炼写作能力,在任务型驱动下对本课以及本单元内容达到灵活运用。

(二) Task 教学设计案例分析

七上 Unit 2 Let's play sports!

Task

Background

It is fun for students to play sports and keep healthy.

Key words: favourite sport, favourite player

Ⅰ Background information

Playing sports is good for our health and popular all over the world. We all like playing sports and have our favourite sports and players. So students should be happy to introduce their hobbies and learn with fun.

Ⅱ Type of the lesson

Task lesson

Ⅲ Teaching aims and learning objectives

By the end of the lesson, the students will be able to:

1. Memorize the new words and phrases.

2. Write an article according to the writing plan.

3. Organize the article with new words, phrases and sentence patterns learnt in this unit.

4. Introduce their favourite sports to others.

Ⅳ Teaching content

1. New words and phrases
2. Writing skills
3. Learn with fun

Ⅴ Focus of the lesson and predicted area of difficulty

1. New words and phrases
2. Organization of the article
3. Application of new words, phrases and sentence patterns
4. How to improve students' involvement in class

Ⅵ Teaching aids

1. Video　2. Pictures　3. Blackboard　4. Chalk
5. Computer　6. Multimedia　7. Projector

Ⅶ Teaching procedures

Step 1 *Warm-up and lead-in*

(1) Play a video and enjoy some pictures of some famous sports players.

【设计理念：1. 教师播放一段录像展示世界著名运动员的风采，活跃课堂气氛，激发学生积极参与课堂的兴趣。2. 师生自由对话，问学生在视频里看到哪些运动员，可以追问学生更多关于运动员的信息。3. 师生自由对话，问学生自己喜欢的运动员并做介绍，增进师生间的了解，创造良好的交流环境，鼓励学生勇于表达自己。】

T: Boys and girls, just now we watched a video of some famous sports players. Who do you see in the video? (可以追问 What is he/she good at? Do you like him/her? Do you know other famous players? Can you say something about them?)

What is your favourite sport?

Who is your favourite player?

Do you often watch his/her matches on TV? (板书 match, on TV 并带读)

(2) Teacher shows some pictures of his hero on PPT and has a free talk with students.

【设计理念：让学生猜测老师喜欢的运动员，激发学生的好奇心，并以此

导入生词,多带读加深学生印象。】

T: Can you guess my favourite player?

T: This is a picture. Who is he?

S: He is Lin Dan.

T: What is he good at?

S: He is good at playing badminton.

T: Yes. And he is a member of the Chinese badminton team. (板书带读 team)

Look! He is playing badminton in a match.

He is many people's hero. (板书带读 hero)

Look! They are all our Chinese people's heroes. (板书带读 heroes)

Step 2 *I love sports*

(1) Students read the article—I love sports and fill in the table.

【设计理念:1. 通过让学生阅读文章,完成相关表格,初步完成对文本内容的梳理。2. 通过问答的方式呈现答案,让学生初步完成对目标话题语言素材的积累。3. 通过学生回答导入四会短语 talk about/of, watch basketball matches。】

T: Just now, we talked about our favourite sports and our heroes. Now I'd like you to meet David. He is a student at Sunshine Middle School. Do you want to know more about him, his favourite sports and hero? Please read the article and complete the table.

David's favourite sport	
His favourite sport	
He is a member of	
He often plays with	
He and his friends often	
His favourite player	

T: Now let's check the answers. What is his favourite sport?

S: His favourite sports is basketball.

T: Which team is he in?

S: He is in his school basketball team.

T：Who does he often play with? And when?

S：He often plays basketball with his friends after school.

T：What do they often do?

S：They often talk about basketball and watch basketball matches on TV.（板书带读 talk about，watch basketball matches）

T：Who is his favourite player?

S：Yao Ming.

（2）Classify the information

【设计理念：1. 通过再次朗读文章，将文章信息进行归纳，学生能掌握每段大意并形成分段意识。2. 老师板书每段大意，为总结常用表达做铺垫。3. 通过听磁带并跟读，学生模仿语音语调，培养语感。】

T：Please read David's article again. Try to classify the information. Put the letters into the brackets.

Paragraph One （ ）

Paragraph Two （ ）

Paragraph Three （ ）

A. What is David's favourite sport?

B. What team is David in?

C. When does David often play basketball?

D. Who does David often play basketball with?

E. What else do David and his friends often do?

F. What do they watch on TV?

G. Who is David's hero?

H. Why does David like Yao Ming?

（核对答案并板书每段大意）

Listen to the tape and read the article.

（3）Discuss useful expressions

【设计理念：学生组内讨论每段能使用的常用表达，写在白板上，然后全班交流展示。老师根据小组展示，提炼每组总结的常用表达，将板书补充完整，来帮助学生对目标话题的常用表达形成知识体系，完成写作前的语言积累。】

T：Now I'd like you to work in groups and discuss useful expressions of each paragraph and write them down on your white board.

（教师根据学生总结得好的表达完善板书）

（4）Pair work

【设计理念：通过使用常用表达谈论自己喜欢的运动和运动员，学生熟练使用目标语言，为接下来的写作奠定基础。】

Students work in pairs and answer questions with useful expressions.

1. What sport do you love/like/enjoy?
2. What is your favourite sport/player?
3. Who do you often play … with?
4. Where do you often play … ?
5. When do you often play … ?
6. Why do you like … ?

Step 3 *Writing*

【设计理念：1. 通过完成书本表格，来完成写作素材的积累。2. 学生根据表格信息和黑板上总结的常用表达和分段写文章。3. 通过让学生互相批改作文，并根据表格里的评分标准打分，让学生相互学习同伴作文中的亮点和好的表达来拓宽思路，并提高自批作文的能力。4. 学生组内讨论推荐一篇文章，老师全班点评。】

（1）Fill in the table in Part B.

T: We have read David's article. Now, can you introduce your favourite sport in the same way? Do you want to try? Please fill in the table in Part B with your own information.

（2）Writing.

Students write an article with the information in the table and useful expressions.

（3）Revision.

Students revise their partners' articles with the help of the table. Then work in groups and choose the best one.

项　目	细　节	分　值
内容(4)	1. 分段描述,结构清晰 2. 信息齐全	1 3
语言(4)	3. 正确使用时态,正确使用连接词 4. 语言正确,无语法错误	1 3
其他(2)	5. 单词拼写正确,大小写、标点使用正确 6. 书写工整,卷面整洁	1 1

(4) Presentation.

Teacher shows the best article of each group and makes comments.

Step 4 *Homework*

【设计理念:1. 通过背诵单词和短语,巩固课堂所学。2. 通过修改作文,学生运用通过交流展示学习到的好的表达和想法,丰富作文内容。】

(1) Remember the new words and phrases.

(2) Revise the article.

Ⅷ　Blackboard design

7A Unit 2 Task

(1) New words and phrases

team　　talk about/of sth.

match　　watch basketball matches

heroes　　make me happy/feel great

(2) Structure

Para. 1: favourite sports

Para. 2: what team; when; who

Para. 3: favourite player

(3) Useful expressions

I like/love/enjoy …

my favourite sport/ …

play … with …

make sb. happy

…

Ⅸ Teaching reflection

本课的主题是写一篇文章介绍自己喜欢的运动和运动员。老师首先播放一段录像展示世界著名运动员的风采,以此来活跃课堂气氛,激发学生的兴趣,让他们能积极参与到课堂中来。然后师生自由对话,谈论在视频里看到的运动员,并追问学生更多关于他们的信息。接下来让学生谈论自己喜欢的运动员并做介绍,来增进师生间的相互了解,创造良好的交流环境,鼓励学生勇于表达自己,为接下来的活动奠定基础。

在处理文本内容时,学生先阅读文章,完成相关表格,然后通过问答的方式呈现答案,导入四会短语。再次朗读文章时,学生将文章信息归纳,掌握每段大意并形成分段意识。以此让学生在整体上对文章的谋篇布局做到心中有数。而语言素材的积累是通过让学生先在组内讨论每段能使用的常用表达,写在白板上交流展示,然后由老师提炼每组总结的常用表达,将板书补充完整,帮助学生形成知识体系。

在学生进行正式写作时,根据自己填写的表格信息和黑板上总结的常用表达写作。写完以后学生互相批改作文,并根据表格里的评分标准打分。这样可以让学生在学习好作文的亮点和表达以及拓宽思路的同时,发现自己在写作方面存在的不足,提高自批自改的能力。

点评:

在2011版的英语课程标准中,对于初中英语写作课的教学目标做出了以下要求:在初中英语写作课中,学生要乐于用书面英语表达意思,能够基本连贯地表述与表达事实、观点、情感,形成基本的写作能力。本节课的设计思路基本达到了以上要求:

写前通过播放相关视频,激发了学生兴趣,并导入了本节课中的重点单词、短语和句型,激活了相关信息。让学生猜测教师所喜爱的运动员及此运动员的相关信息,更将课堂推入了一个小高潮,再次激发学生的兴趣,并对本节课中的重要表达有了初步的接触。写中通过填表格、回答问题、写提纲、归纳段落大意,既再一次导入新的短语,又让学生深刻理解了范文,学生的段落意识也得到进一步提升。组内总结写作常用表达并写在黑板上,通过小组竞争的方式,以看似游戏的方式,不仅将课堂氛围推向了最高潮,也在无形中帮助学生掌握了重要表达。写后以学生互助的形式帮助学生修改错误,提高写作能力。

整节课主线明确,过渡自然,衔接巧妙,内容丰富扎实,操练形式多样,并做到了以学生为中心,也发挥了教师指导、示范、启发、鼓励的作用。写作评价方式多样化。但建议加强课堂的趣味性,采用游戏、竞猜、竞争等多种形式,去激发学生的积极性,培养学生竞争与合作的精神。另在课堂升华部分须再多下些功夫。

七下 Unit 6 Outdoor fun
Task
More of *Alice in Wonderland*

Background

Teacher lives in a magic world. Everything has magic.

Key words: magic cup, magic water, magic cake, magic pens

Ⅰ Background information

Alice in Wonderland is a very famous book for children written by Lewis Carroll, which is loved by many people. The writer had great imagination. The book is full of strange things. Students in 7th grade are also imaginative, so they must be very interested in writing their own *Alice in Wonderland*.

Ⅱ Type of the lesson

Writing lesson

Ⅲ Teaching aims and learning objectives

By the end of the lesson, the students will be able to:

1. Understand the meanings of the new words.
   Use them in proper situations.
2. Imagine the developing of their own *Alice in Wonderland*.
3. Describe a story to others clearly.
4. Use the simple past tense to write a story.
5. Cooperate with partners and experience the feeling of success.

Ⅳ Teaching content

1. New words
2. The story of a sample writing
3. Different writing skills

Ⅴ Focus of the lesson and predicted area of difficulty

1. New words and the story of the sample writing
2. Different writing skills
3. How to lead students to imagine

Ⅵ Teaching aids

1. Cup 2. Water 3. Blackboard 4. Chalk
5. Computer 6. Multimedia 7. Projector

Ⅶ Teaching procedures

Step 1 *Magic cup* (*Warm-up and lead-in*)

(1) Play a song and enjoy some pictures about magic before class.

【设计理念：1. 通过教师制作的关于魔术的 video 导入两个生词(decide, enter)。2. 用师生对话活跃课堂气氛，让学生对神秘的事情产生好奇心，调动学生参与下一个环节的积极性。】

T：Do you like the song? Do you like the pictures?

What can you see in the picture? Do you love magic?

Can you play magic? Do you believe I can play magic? Yes, because I am a magician! Today, I decide to take you to go into a magic world. (板书带读 decide). If you enter(板书，带读) the magic world, you will find that everything has magic.

(2) Play magic(变魔术).

【设计理念：1. 通过教师自己表演的魔术导入重要的结构 too ... to ... 和生词 fail。2. 用魔术激发学生的好奇心和参与课堂的积极性。3. 通过询问学生水去了哪里过渡到 magic water。】

T：Do you want to enter(重复操练) the magic world with me? OK, here we go! What's this? Yes, it's a magic cup. Look, I put some water into it. Do you want to drink the water? No! Because it's too cold to(板书，带读) drink.

OK, what will really happen? Please look at the cup very carefully. I hope I can do it and I won't fail(带读，板书). Is it magic? Will you give me a big hand? Thank you very much! But the problem is where the water is. Do you want to know? Let me tell you. It is here on the table. Is it magic water? Yes, it is.

(3) Review the reading part and move to this lesson.

【设计理念：1. 简单复习 Reading 课文，让学生对故事的发展有系统的认识，帮助学生更好地理解下面的故事，为最后的写作做铺垫。2. 利用 magic water 引入到 task 文本。3. 导入 small enough to ... 句型。4. 操练之前的生词和句型。】

T：And she saw magic water. Who is she? Yes, she is Alice! In the reading part, we learned that Alice followed the rabbit into a big hole. Then she saw a very small door. Outside the door, she found a very beautiful garden. Right? Could she enter(重复操练) the garden? Why?（找一个学生回答）

Yes, she was too big, or I can say the door was too small.

She was not smaller enough(导入句型，齐读) to enter the door.

She was too big to enter the door(重复操练 too ... to ... 结构).

So she failed(重复操练).

Step 2 *Magic water (Solve the reading story)*

(1) Did Alice drink the water? What happened to her after that?

【设计理念：1. 通过问题导读的方式引导学生阅读第一、第二段关于喝完水的变化，找出文章中的 magic things。2. 处理文本内容，梳理情节发展。】

T：Then she found magic water here. Did she drink the water? What happened to her after that? OK, please turn your book to Page 78. Read Paras. 1–2 carefully and find what magic(突出主线) things happened to her.

T：Are you ready? Let me check your answers.（对答案）

(2) Did she go through the door? Why?（处理 3、4 段）

【设计理念：1. 通过问题导读的方式引导学生阅读第三、第四段关于主人公身体变化之后发生的事情以及心理的变化。2. 详细处理文本内容，梳理情节发展，给学生留下深刻印象，增强他们想象的主动性。】

T：Was she small enough to enter the door? But did she enter(重复操练 enter) the garden? Why? Please read Para. 3 and find the answers.

T：Did you find the answers? Hands up! She didn't enter the garden, because she forgot about the key on the table. Could she reach the key? No, because she was too short to reach the key(重复操练 too ... to ...).

T：But she found something under the table. What was it? Please read the last paragraph.

T：What was it? A piece of cake!

（3）Read and match.（To get the structure of the story）

【设计理念：1. 提纲挈领，分析文章的结构，了解范文在写作过程中是如何分段的，为自己接下来的写作做好铺垫。2. 引导学生分段处理故事情节，抓住每个段落的大意。】

T：There are four paragraphs in the story. And I will show you the pictures of each one. Please read the story again very quickly and match the picture with the paragraph.

T：I think it's very easy for you. Let me check your answers. You did a great job. Boys and girls, from Paras. 1－4, can you see the developing of the story? Yes, so when we write a story, we also need to tell others the developing of the story in different paragraphs.

（3）Talk about the writing skills in the sample writing.

【设计理念：1. 引导学生进行细节描写，润色情节，为故事增加一定的色彩。2. 引导学生正确使用连词，如 and, but, however 等保证语句通顺，以及使用过渡句，增强段落之间的连贯性。3. 学会使用副词，让故事生动。】

T：For example, in the second paragraph, Alice drank the water, and her body became bigger and bigger. Let's read the sentences together. OK, now let's read the whole second paragraph together. Which story do you like? The first one or the second one? Why? Yes, the second one is interesting. The first one is not interesting. So if you want to make your story interesting. Please write some details.

T：The story is interesting. But we still can make it more interesting. For example, let's read this sentence together. But this time, boys and girls, think carefully. Did she drink it very slowly or quickly? Why? Then let's come to this one. Quickly or slowly? Why? Yes, we have lots of adverbs to use. Let's read them together.

T：Now, let's come to these two sentences. Read them together. Did I lose one word? Which one? Read them again. Which one is better? So when we write two sentences, sometimes we can use some conjunctions to make it better. What other conjunctions do you know? Good! Please remember to use them.

T：The story is interesting. But we still can make it more interesting. For example, let's read this sentence together. But this time, boys and girls, think carefully. Did she drink it very slowly or quickly? Why? Then let's come to this one. Quickly or slowly? Why? Yes, we have lots of adverbs to use. Let's read them together.

（4）Fill in the blanks：Use the writing skills to rewrite the sample writing.

【设计理念：1. 回顾 Task 故事情节。2. 巩固写作技能的使用。3. 导入 magic cake。】

T：Now, boys and girls. let's me check if you still remember the stroy and if you can use the writing skills very well.

T：Who can tell me the answers? Your did a good job! Let's read the last sentence together.

Step 3 *Magic cake*（*Imagine for writing*）

（2）Discuss：What will happen if she eats the cake?

【设计理念：1. 以教师的想象为例子，打开学生思维，激发学生想象，而不是只局限于原小说的故事情节。2. 集思广益，为写作丰富资源。3. 同时为接下来的 Pair work 做铺垫。】

T：Yes, she found the cake under the table. Is it a magic cake? Will she eat the cake? What will happen after that? Will she fly? Will she become bigger and bigger? …（教师给出两个很出乎意料的变化）Do you have some interesting and amazing ideas? Now, please discuss with your partner. And you can tell me after that.

T：How many of you think that Alice will eat the cake?（找一个学生回答）How many of you think that Alice won't eat the cake?（找一个学生回答）

（3）Pair work：（Talk about the five questions）

【设计理念：1. 讨论书后出现的 5 个问题，通过对话丰富写作资源。2. 相互借鉴写作资源，鼓励想象力丰富的学生扩充问题，可以询问 5 个问题以外的其他细节问题。3. 为接下来的 Group work 做好铺垫。】

T：Different people have different answers. Please work in pairs and talk about the five questions with your partner.（找两组）

(3) Group work: Tell a story (Who has the most interesting one?)

【设计理念：1. 以小组合作的方式，尝试用过去式讲述简短故事，强化时态的正确性。2. 增加故事的细节问题，在一定程度上形成口头作文，鼓励学生讲述，为写作做铺垫。3. 组内选出本组最有趣的故事，为小组合作写作收集最优的资源。】

T: You have interesting ideas. Now I want you to tell your story to your group members. But when you tell a story, you have to use the simple past tense. And tell others more like … Are you clear? Now, try to find whose is the most interesting one.

T: OK, whose story is the most interesting one in your group? (找一组询问) Would you please tell your story to us?

Step 4 *Magic pens* (*Write their own stories*)

【设计理念：1. 写作前引导学生分段，便于在写作过程中有更清楚的思路。2. 提供重点的写作句型和短语。3. 引导能力较强的学生写出过渡段落，甚至更多故事情节。】

T: Just now, you tell me great stories, but if I ask you to write the stories, how many paragraphs are you going to write?

T: Yes, three. But if you have some more time, you can write another paragraph before Para. 1 and more after Para. 3. Are you clear?

T: Good. Will you be a good writer? Of course, Lorries Carrel has a magic pen. You also have magic pens. Please use your magic pens to take us into a magic world! Now, work in group, choose one to write, and the others just give advice. (开始写作)

Step 5 *How to appraise a good writing*(点评作文)

【设计理念：1. 通过教师引导学生的作文批改提纲，从篇章到段落再到语法，理解如何去评价作文。2. 同学之间学会自评、互评，有利于学生在以后的作文书写前形成规范的格式。3. 欣赏好的文章，学以致用。】

T: Before reading your story, I will tell you how to appraise a good writing …

T: Today we had a great time together in a magic world. Are you happy? Me too. With your imagination, your life will be full of magic every day. So keep it because it is very important for you!

Step 5 *Homework*

【设计理念：1. 在小组合作的基础上，开始个人写作，巩固课堂所学。2. 引导对写作感兴趣的同学，自己进行创作、改编。】

T：Now please remember your homework：

(1) Write the story by yourself and share with each other.

(2) Choose one of your favourite novels(小说) and try to write more after it.

Ⅷ Blackboard design

7B Unit 6 Outdoor fun—Task

More of *Alice in Wonderland*

magic	Paragraph 1
decide	Paragraph 2
enter	Paragraph 3

Ⅸ Teaching reflection

本节课主要通过几个与魔力有关的环节将教学分成四个不同的部分，分别是 magic cup，magic water，magic cake，magic pens。由老师所做的倒入杯中的水消失的魔术，导入到消失的水去哪了，进入本节课的第二个部分 magic water，从而处理教材所提供的这篇范文。处理过程包含两个部分：第一是了解各段落的大意，第二是从范文中提炼写作技巧，包括形容词、副词、连词、过渡等，让学生学会在写作过程中润色文本。第二部分结束后从桌子上的蛋糕开始引导学生想象吃完蛋糕之后所发生的事情，也就进入了本节课的第三个环节 magic cake，本部分主要以 pair work 和 group work 为主让学生在有层次的活动中展开想象的翅膀，最终形成口头作文。最后一个部分就是 magic pens，用有魔力的笔写出好的作文。

本节课在环节设计上比较紧凑，内容也比较多。尤其是在第三个部分，活动较多，学生能展示的机会不是很充分，在用过去时讲故事的时候，只能叫一组展示，其他组的同学虽然准备充分，但是没有时间来展示，也是本节课的遗憾。还有很多同学受到原著的影响，想象力没有打开，也是在以后的教学中教师要深刻思考的问题。

点评：

不同于其他课型，task 最终以“产品形式”——作文呈现出来，学生最终的作文可以直接反映出本节课的效果。本课时与以往的 Task 还略有不同，它是在基于已有故事情景的基础上进行的续写，因此，积极开发学生的想象力成为本节课的一个重点与难点。

本课可以算作一节优课，比较好地完成了教学目标，学生最终在情境内通过想象，完成了一篇续写。本课主线明晰，magic 一词贯穿全文，逐层递进，开始便将学生带入魔法的世界，为之后的想象和写作提供情境，并自然导入了生词，适时进行操练。但开头的魔术略显多余，学生本身就很熟悉爱丽丝的魔法世界，变魔术有些偏离情境。本节课有 3 个亮点。首先，篇章意识很强，对文本分段处理。关注文本细节，引导学生关注不同连词的作用，在作文中正确使用，使逻辑更紧密。其次，点评很人性化。在学生发言后，不仅关注知识点评，还有内容和情感方面的评价。最后，引入学生互评的活动，提供评价标准，既加强了学生间的学习与合作，也为学生写作提供了参照，但是标准还有待细化与精确。

本节课在启发学生思考和开发学生想象力方面还有待加强。magic cake 以及之后的一连串反问，限制了学生的思维，学生想象力被局限，多想到吃完蛋糕后变大变小、会飞等内容，大同小异，没有太多个性，没有充分发挥想象，导致之后的写作出现较多的雷同情况。建议为学生提供更多的情境，而不是局限在某一点上。并且要采用各种方式，让学生积极思考、联想、想象，创造自己的个性故事。

八上　Unit 4　Do it yourself

Task

A DIY story

Background

Many people like DIY nowadays. They have different interesting DIY experiences.

Key words: birthday salad, birthday card, more DIY stories

I　Background information

DIY is very popular among people all over the world now. It is easy and convenient to do it. And it can save money and bring a lot of happiness to people. Some people like to make DIY presents when someone's birthday is coming. And they have many interesting and unforgettable DIY experiences. Students in Grade 8 must have some wonderful DIY experiences.

Ⅱ Type of the lesson

Writing lesson

Ⅲ Teaching aims and learning objectives

By the end of the lesson, the students will be able to:

1. Understand the meanings of the new words.
   Use them in proper situations.
2. Share their DIY experiences with their classmates.
3. Write a diary to record what he has done.
4. Use the simple past tense to keep a diary.
5. Cooperate with partners and experience the feeling of success.

Ⅳ Teaching content

1. New words
2. The story of a sample writing
3. Different writing skills

Ⅴ Focus of the lesson and predicted area of difficulty

1. New words and the diary of the sample writing
2. Different writing skills
3. How to lead students to describe their DIY experiences

Ⅵ Teaching aids

1. Blackboard 2. Chalk 3. Computer
4. Multimedia 5. Projector 6. Card

Ⅶ Teaching procedures

Step 1 *Birthday salad* (*Warm-up and lead-in*)

Play a short video about some classmates who are making fruit salad.

(1) Birthday salad

【设计理念:1. 观看视频后,从视频内容出发,老师通过问问题,学生回答,师生交流,导入生词和词组(keep it secret, have fun, complete, go wrong, cover),为之后理解范文做准备。2. 用师生对话活跃课堂气氛,调动学生参与的积极性。】

T: When someone's birthday is coming, what will you do?

Maybe we can make some presents by ourselves. These students made some gifts by themselves. Do you know these students? What did they do in the video? Why did they do this?

Yes, they made fruit salad for their teacher's birthday. And they kept it secret. So their teacher didn't know it. It was a big surprise.

Did they do alone?

No, they worked together. They had fun working together(板书带读).

Do you know how long it took them to complete(板书带读) it?

It took them one hour. So long, right? Because many things went wrong(板书带读).

After completing, what can you see on the cover(板书带读) of the book?

(2) Birthday card beside the salad

【设计理念:1. 此处老师现场演示如何将一张空白的卡片变成漂亮的生日贺卡,在制作的过程中,导入生词和词组(balloon, stick, paint, spell, cut out),为之后理解范文做准备。2. 用师生对话活跃课堂气氛,调动学生参与积极性。3. 为学生之后讨论和写作提供素材。】

And they wanted to give it to their teacher as a birthday present. (Take out a card with nothing on it) So they made a birthday card and put it beside it. How was the card?

Yes, it was boring. So what should the students do then?

They cut out a picture of balloons(板书带读) and painted(板书带读) them different colours. And then they stuck(板书带读) the picture on it. How was it?

Much better.

And they should also write something on it. What should they write?

Yes, happy birthday. And they should spell(板书带读) the words correctly.

Step 2 *Birthday card(Solve the sample writing)*

(1) Our friend Suzy also made a card for her mother.

【设计理念:1. 阅读全文,通过回答与文章内容有关的问题,从而了解日记的大概内容。2. 递进式的问题展现了故事如何展开,学生回答后可以熟悉如何描述一个故事。】

T：Our friend Suzy also made a card. Why did she made the card? Why didn't she make it at home? Did Sandy help? What mistakes did Suzy keep making? What colour did Suzy use for the roses?

T：Are you ready? Let me check your answers.（对答案）

（2）Read and match.（To get the structure of the story）

【设计理念：1. 阅读文章后，提纲挈领，分析文章的结构，得出每段大意。2. 引导学生学会分段处理故事的叙述。3. 为之后写作提供结构框架，做好铺垫。】

T：There are four paragraphs in the story. Can you tell me the main idea of each paragraph?

T：I think it's very easy for you. Let me check your answers.

Para. 1：The reason why Suzy made a birthday card.

Para. 2：How she made the card.

Para. 3：What happened in the end.

Para. 4：Suzy's hope.

（3）Talk about the writing skills in the sample writing.

【设计理念：1. 通过引导学生关注关键动词及动词短语，使其关注动词在详细过程描写中的作用。2. 引导学生关注不同连词的作用，在写作时正确使用连词，保证逻辑性。】

T：For example, in the third paragraph, I coloured. I also cut out ... and stuck ... Let's read the sentences together. OK, so you can see some verbs and verb phrases here. By reading these, we can have a clear idea about how to make this card more beautiful.

T：Now, let's come to these two sentences. Mum's birthday is coming.（So）I decided to make her ... Read them together. Did I lose one word? Which one? Read them again. Which one is better? So when we write two sentences, sometimes we can use some conjunctions to make it better. What other conjunctions do you know? Good! Please remember to use them.

（4）Pair work.

【设计理念：1. 回顾 Task 日记内容，检测学生对于关键表达的掌握情况。2. 巩固写作技能的使用。3. 导入 birthday ice cream，为之后学生自己谈

论 DIY 经历做准备。】

T: Now, boys and girls, let me check if you still remember how Suzy made the card and if you can use the writing skills very well. Now suppose one is Suzy, the other wants to know something about it.

Model:

A: Hi, Suzy. I heard you made a card for your mother. Why did you make the card?

Suzy: I ...

A: Where did you make it?

Suzy: I ... Because ...

A: How did you make it?

Suzy: I ... and Sandy ...

A: Did you make any mistakes?

Suzy: Yes, I ...

A: What else did you do?

Suzy: I ... and ...

A: You are so great! I hope ...

Step 3 *DIY experiences (Offering materials for writing)*

(4) Lead-in: Birthday ice cream

【设计理念：1. 以教师 DIY 经历作为示范，打开学生思维。2. 导入一些新的表达，为学生之后的写作输入丰富资源。3. 为正式写作前的 pair work 做铺垫。】

T: Last Sunday was my sister's birthday. Do you know how we celebrated her birthday?

I made mango ice cream for her. Do you want to know how I made it?

T: I made it last Saturday. And my friend helped me. We had fun making it together.

First, I needed to prepare something. (show a picture) What did I prepare?

Milk, eggs, sugar, cream, and magazines.

Then what should I do?

I cut the mangoes into pieces, mixed the sugar and eggs, stirred them until it turned white. What was next?

I cooked the milk. But I made a mistake. I cooked it for a long time. So there was milk anywhere.

Then I added milk to the eggs and sugar. And then I added mangoes to them. I put it into the fridge. How was the ice cream? How was my DIY experience?

(5) Pair work (Talk about their DIY experiences)

【设计理念：1. 通过对话，让学生学会如何口头描述自己的 DIY 经历，为正式写作做准备。2. 通过倾听他人的 DIY 经历，相互借鉴写作资源。3. 为小组讨论 DIY 经历的 group work 做铺垫。】

T: Different people have different DIY experiences. Please work in pairs and talk about your DIY experiences with your partner.（两组学生展示）

(6) Group work: Share the DIY story (who has the most interesting DIY story).

【设计理念：1. 让学生尝试用过去时来讲述发生在过去的简短故事或经历。2. 通过小组讨论，组内选出本组最有趣的故事，为小组合作写作收集最优资源。】

T: You have interesting DIY experiences. Now I want you to tell your story to your group members. But when you tell a story, you have to use the simple past tense. And tell others more like ... Are you clear? Now, try to find whose is the most interesting one.

T: OK, whose story is the most interesting one in your group?（找一组询问）Would you please tell your story to us?

Step 4 *Your DIY story (Write their own stories)*

【设计理念：1. 写作前引导学生增强分段意识。2. 提供写作有用的表达。3. 引导能力较强的学生写出更详细的故事情节。】

T: Just now, you tell me great stories, but if I ask you to write the stories, how many paragraphs are you going to write?

T: Yes, three.

T: Good, wish you be a good writer.（开始写作）

Step 5 *How to appraise a good writing*（点评作文）

【设计理念：1. 通过呈现评价标准的表格，帮助学生理解如何去评价作文。2. 让学生根据评价标准，学会自评，并优化作文。3. 让小组成员间互评，学生学会欣赏他人的长处，并取长补短。】

T: Before reading your story, I will tell you how to appraise a good writing …

T: Today we had a great time together. Are you happy? Me too. DIY is really interesting and can bring us a lot of happiness. So you can do more DIY jobs after class to make yourself and others happy.

Step 6 *Homework*

【设计理念：1. 在小组合作的基础上，开始个人写作，巩固课堂所学。2. 引导对写作感兴趣的同学，课后自我优化。】

T: Now please remember your homework:

（1）Write the story by yourself and share it with each other.

（2）Try to make your writing better after class.

Ⅷ Blackboard design:

8A Unit 4 Do it yourself—Task

A DIY story

<table>
<tr><td rowspan="8">Reason
How
Hope</td><td>keep it secret</td><td rowspan="8">Verbs/Verb phrases</td></tr>
<tr><td>have fun working together</td></tr>
<tr><td>It takes … to complete</td></tr>
<tr><td>go wrong</td></tr>
<tr><td>paint balloon(s) + different colors</td></tr>
<tr><td>cut out</td></tr>
<tr><td>stick—stuck</td></tr>
<tr><td>spell (spelt) the words</td></tr>
</table>

Ⅸ Teaching reflection

本节课为 Task 课型，主要目的是培养孩子的写作技能。通过对课本中范文的结构、写作技巧以及有用的表达等学习后，自己根据实际情况写出自己的故事。平时孩子写作机会不多，且关于 DIY 的经历也较为贫乏，即使有，也不善表达，因此要写出一篇 DIY 的文章对于学生略有难度，所以在写作之前需要大量的信息输入，为学生提供写作资源与示范，例如，刚开始的导入 birthday salad, birthday card 以及后面的 birthday ice cream，都是此用意。

本节课在上完以后，我感觉有以下不足，需要改进。

① 在导入部分，以本校学生制作沙拉的视频导入，虽比较贴近学生的生活，但因为不是本班学生的制作经历，学生并没有表现出特别的热情。导入如果可以以学生自己的生活和学习经历导入，学生的参与热情应该会更高，也更有共鸣。② 在导入部分，导入了很多生词和短语，但是操练略显不足，学生对于这些知识点如何运用仍然不是很了解。且知识点多是老师呈现，教师需要探求一种由学生积极参与呈现新知识的模式，这对于学生的预习工作提出了较高的要求。同时，在导入部分，老师对于学生的提问无太多技术含量，对于打开学生思维的效果仍然不够理想。③ 对于范文的处理，尤其是在挖掘写作技巧时，处理有些仓促。如让学生关注动词和动词短语时，应该让学生去找出能反映如何制作生日卡片的单词和短语，让学生自己去发现动词对于描述事件过程的重要性。

点评：

课堂教学设计理念新。这位教师上课运用任务型教学方式引导学生积极参与教学活动。在导入过程中实现师生、生生互动，活动内容丰富多彩，接近学生生活，在互动、交流、合作、探究中实施教学。整个过程中教师的角色起了深刻的变化，真正成了组织者、参与者、引导者、帮助者，关注学生学习策略、学习方法、学习态度，成为名副其实的“以学为本”的教学设计者。

体现了新课程的目标。这位老师在教学过程中处理好“知识与技能、过程与方法、情感态度与价值观之间的关系”。是教书本，而是以书本教，以学生现有的知识经验导入，从开始的做生日卡片到做水果沙拉，这些都和学生密切相关，由学习课本的语言知识输入到延伸过程中的语言知识输出，通过教师引导使学生运用语言知识，学会交际，学会做事情。例：So what should the students do then? 运用学到的语言知识学会做事，这就是能力。重视情感态度与价值观的培养。教师在教学过程中，教授学生制作水果沙拉。教学过程中培养学生的团队合作精神，积极调动不同层次学生积极学习，自主学习，积极评价，激发持续的学习热情，不断使学生体验成功，提高学生的自我价值，也注重了个性的培养。

不足之处：这节课在二次导入的时候引入了芒果冰淇淋的制作步骤，学生虽然对这个比较感兴趣,但是因为不能亲自体验而降低了趣味性。单纯的图片和文字并不能给学生留下深刻的印象。如果教师能真正地让学生参与制作,自己 DIY 一份芒果冰淇淋,这样效果可能来的更明显一点,并且也能更加充实学生的作文,让学生有话可说。

八下 Unit 7 International charities

Task

Background

There are many international charities in the world. They help the people in need in different ways. Students will develop the idea of trying to help the charities.

Key words: international charities

Ⅰ Background information

There are many international charities in the world. They help the people in need in different ways. In this unit, students will know five international charities. They are UNICEF, Oxfam, World Vision, ORBIS and WWF.

Ⅱ Type lesson

Task

Ⅲ Teaching aims

By the end of the lesson, students should be able to:

1. Memorize the new words and phrases.

2. Write an article according to a writing plan.

3. Organize the article with new words, phrases and sentence patterns learnt in this unit.

4. Introduce an Indian girl's life in the past and at present.

Ⅳ Teaching content

1. New words and phrases

2. Writing skills

Ⅴ Focus of the lesson and predicted area of difficulty

1. New words and phrases

2. Writing material collection

3. Writing skills

Ⅵ Teaching aids

1. Video 2. Pictures 3. Blackboard 4. Chalk
5. Computer 6. Multimedia 7. Projector

Ⅶ Teaching procedures

Step 1 *Warm-up and lead-in (about 3 – 5 mins.)*

Activity 1: *Revision about ORBIS*—(about 2 mins.)

T: Let's look at this picture. What does this logo stand for?

S: ORBIS.

T: How does ORBIS help?

S: It uses its Flying Eye Hospital to visit poor areas. On it, volunteer doctors do operations.

T: Would you like to be one of them?

S: ...

T: Diana is a nurse from ORBIS. Let's look at some pictures about the changes in Diana's life.

(Present some pictures.)

【设计理念：教师通过呈现 ORBIS 的图片来导入话题，与学生进行自由交流，帮助学生复习关于慈善的相关内容。通过师生、生生之间的对话和形式多样的学习方式加强学生对所学内容的理解和掌握。主要采用了问题情景法，问题的设置由浅入深，并富于启发性和拓展性，目的在于促进学生的思维。按照"吸收信息—处理和加工信息—口/笔头表达信息"的思路对学生进行写作技能的训练。在与学生 free talk 中，导入一些生词和短语，并引出女孩 Diana，为下一个环节的进行做铺垫。】

Step 2 *Presentation (about 5 – 6 mins.)*

T: Let's look at the first two pictures. What was Diana's job?

S: She was a secretary of a company.

T: So she is an office lady. Does she look happy?

S: No.

T: Which does Diana like better? Travelling by car or by plane?

S: By car.

T: Why? Can you have a guess?

S: Because she was afraid of travelling by plane.

T: Let's look at these two pictures. Can you describe the two pictures with your own words?

S: She is working as an ORBIS nurse. She helps doctors do an operation. She is getting used to travelling by plane. She is glad to help people see again.

T: Is she happy now?

S: Yes.

T: But what made her decide to be a nurse for ORBIS? What happened? Please open your books and find out the reasons.

S: ...

T: Please use "one day ... " to give me the reasons.

S: ... see a programme and knew about ORBIS. After work, she attended courses to work as a nurse.

T: What do you think of Diana?

S: Helpful, clever ...

Picture 1: Diana was a secretary of a company, but she did not feel happy.

Picture 2: Diana was afraid of travelling by plane.

Picture 3: Diana learned about ORBIS on TV.

Picture 4: Diana went to school for special training as a nurse.

Pictures 5 - 6: Diana works for ORBIS now and she looks happy.

【设计理念：通过观看 Diana 过去和现在生活的图片来帮助学生更好地了解她的生活状况。通过描述图片，学生们可以学会使用本课所学的生词、短语和句子来表达他们的观点。通过完成这个任务，生生之间进行了大量的语言交际。在教师的指导下，学生在特定的情境中，通过协作、会话从而有效地完成意义的建构，并体验了通过合作给他们带来的成功的喜悦。】

Step 3 *Changes in Diana's life (about 5 mins.)*

T: Fill in the table about her life.

Changes in Diana's life	
In the past	worked as a secretary was afraid of flying
	learnt about ORBIS on TV
	trained as a nurse and attended courses after work
At present	gets used to travelling by plane enjoys being able to help people see again makes her life more meaningful

【设计理念：通过完成图表，提炼信息，帮助学生更好地组织写作材料，形成较强的逻辑思维，为文章结构的划分打下基础。】

Step 4 *Read and summarize the structure* (*about 5 mins.*)

T：Please read the passage and pay attention to the red parts. What's the function of them?

S：To show the time order.

T：Which are good sentences?

S： …

T：What does each paragraph tell us?

S： …

T：

Paragraph. 1：What was Diana's life like in the past?

Paragraph. 2：What changed Diana's life?

Paragraph. 3：What is she getting used to now?

Paragraph. 4：What does Diana think about her new life?

【设计理念：与表格相呼应，通过这个教学环节来帮助学生掌握文章结构，学习如何组织信息，为下一步的写作做好准备。】

Step 5 *Writing* (*about 20 mins.*)

Look at the pictures and put them in a story

1. Mandeep's life in the past

2. Changes

3. Mandeep's life at present

T：Here's some information about Mandeep's life. Please read it and try to make an outline about it.

Background Mandeep's life in the past changes Mandeep's life at present Mandeep's hopes

S: Background: from India, has many children, poor

Mandeep's life in the past: used to work on the farm all day, couldn't read or write

Changes: a VNICEF office came; learn about … ; help …

Mandeep's life at present: enter a school, can read and write

Mandeep's hopes: to become a teacher

T: Use the phrases and words to make sentences and work in groups to say sth. about her life.

S: …

T: Write your passage.

S: …

T: Please pay attention to the writing criteria.

S: …

T: Revise your partners' report with the help of the table.

【设计理念：通过当堂写作提升学生表达慈善话题的能力，正确使用本单元的词汇与短语；学生还可以通过修改完善同伴的作文来改进自己的作文，同时向他人学习一些好的表达方式。】

Step 6 *Conclusions (1 min.)*

The word needs charity.

Charity can make lives better, not only for those people who get help but also for those people who give help.

【设计理念：任何课程学习的过程中都应该渗透思想和道德情感教育。本单元话题是一个很好的抓手，我们可以利用这一契机对学生进行人性的教育，让学生从小树立正确的人生观，学会关爱他人，鼓励学生帮助需要帮助的人，热心于慈善。】

Step 7 *Homework*

1. Perfect your writing.

2. Remember the new words and phrases.

【设计理念：通过完善作文来提升学生写作能力并学会正确使用本单元的一些生词、短语和句型。】

Ⅷ Blackboard design

Unit 7 Task

In the past	a secretary be afraid of sth./doing sth.
One day	watch ... attend courses
At present	work as a nurse

teach ...

be/get used to doing ...

Ⅸ Teaching reflection

本课是本单元的中心任务，它既是对本单元前面所学知识的综合运用，也是将之前一个阶段知识输入的一次整体性输出的过程和平台。整个过程分为三步：Pre-writing，While-writing 和 Post-writing。其中最重要的应该是第一步 Pre-writing，通过复习国际慈善组织的相关信息，导入本课的主题，充分运用图片，让学生根据图片信息及一些关键词来描述 Diana 的生活变化，这样的口头操练为学生的写作打好基础，让学生先进行口头作文，帮他们理清写作思路。在第二步 While-writing 过程中，再次强调了写作的注意点，如段落结构、人称时态、关联词等，并提供相关的信息给较弱的学生以帮助，要求较好的学生增添信息并用好词句。第三步 Post-writing 中 revising 是较满意的部分，通过教师示范评改、分组评改、展示学生的评改，最后展示教师精心完成的范文，让学生感知什么是好文章，有再写一篇好文章的愿望，为 Re-writing 打好基础。整个过程符合学生的认知规律，循序渐进地教学，重视学生口头运用能力的发展。

在教学的各个环节中，关注学生情感教育，将“帮助他人，热心慈善”的情感目标不知不觉地灌输给学生，通过 free talk 营造轻松的学习氛围，为提高学习效率奠定了基础。

本节课的不足之处在于：

1. 写前阶段的处理过于仓促。这部分应该是本课的重中之重，让学生充分地输入相关的信息和词组，多花点时间让学生自主谈论关于各个慈善组织的相关信息，谈论一些参与慈善的人的生活，并能加入一些自己的感想，为后面的写作打好坚实的基础。

2. 给学生的留白时间太短。提问后及讨论后要给学生充分的时间想一想，不能过于着急地呈现下一步，要增强学生的思维力度。在口头作文时，如果能激发学生的想象力，加入一些更具体的事例细节，学生在描述时应该能更深入、更透彻、更完善。

3. 问题设置缺乏深入思考，学生参与的热情有待提高。学生能够积极地参与到简单的回答和讨论中，但对于一些开放性的问题和小组活动，有些学生仍然胆怯不敢举手，这是由老师铺垫不够和问题设置不够合理导致的。因此必须从平时的每一节课就深入研究，精心备课，注重学生的参与，增强学生的自信，让他们乐于学英语，敢于说英语！

点评：

Task 是每一个单元的高潮部分，是对整个单元的汇总、综合和提升，需要学生具备一定层次的多方面的语言素质，旨在培养学生的写作能力。简而言之，就是以写作的方式，要求学生综合运用本单元所学的知识和获得的技能，完成特定的任务，形成对一个单元的终极成果的展示，即“在学中用，在用中学，为用而学”。8B Unit 7 International charities Task 紧扣本单元的话题，讨论了国际慈善的问题。通过本节课的学习，要求学生了解 ORBIS 志愿者的学习和工作情况，按逻辑顺序整理思路，根据图片和提纲中的信息，写一篇关于一个印度女孩的受助报告。

为了引入话题，吸引学生的兴趣，作者采用了问题情景法。只有精心设计的活动才能激发学生的热情。学生的兴趣被激活时，他们才有内驱力和创造力，才能发挥出最佳水平。作者通过图片让学生有了先行一步的视觉冲击，然后由此引发出来的问题，学生自然而然会有兴趣探索，从而点燃整节课的导火线，为下面的流光溢彩做好铺垫。

有效的写作教学需要以话题为主线，在导入、训练、巩固和拓展环节中，力求做到由简到繁，由易到难，前后相连，层层深入，让学生可以在真实的环境中操练并且愉快地学习。作者的话题是慈善，目标是写一篇受助的印度女孩的报告。整个课堂设计思路虽简单清晰，但是并没有在一个大的情景下去安排每一个部分的内容,环节与环节之间太过独立和零散,缺少主线的穿针引线。学生要想有很好的语言输出,那么必然要有充分的语言输入,可就上课的流程来看,操练的部分较少,没有足够的语言输入,这一点需要作者再做思考和改进。

九上 Unit 2 Colours

Task

Background

Teacher helps students to do a project on the relationship between people's moods and colours.

Key words: colours, moods

I Background information

Some surveys say that there is a relationship between colours and moods. Each colour may represent some special moods. As a result, people can change their moods by choosing different colours to wear. Students in Grade 9 are very curious and they have the ability to do some research, so they must be very interested in writing their discovery of the relationship between colours and moods.

II Type of the lesson

Writing lesson

III Teaching aims and learning objectives

By the end of the lesson, the students will be able to:

1. Understand the meanings of the new words.
   Use them in proper situations.
2. Review and grasp some common colours and what they represent.
3. Organize their ideas before writing with the help of a table.
4. Write a report using what they've learned according to the writing instruction and standards.
5. Cooperate with partners and use proper colours to change moods.

IV Teaching content

1. New words
2. The table and the sample writing

3. Different writing skills

Ⅴ Focus of the lesson and predicted area of difficulty

1. New words and the structure of the sample writing

2. Different writing skills

3. How to lead students to imagine and create

Ⅵ Teaching aids

1. Blackboard 2. Chalk 3. Computer 4. Multimedia 5. Projector

Ⅶ Teaching procedures

Step 1 *Free talk and lead-in*

(1) Play a video about the London Fashion Show to lead in the topic of colors.

【设计理念：因为本课写作对象为两则广告的模特，故而选用伦敦时装秀，让学生融入情境。课前播放的视频能迅速激起学生对于颜色的兴趣，并引入话题。】

T: Good morning, boys and girls. Just now, when you watched the video, many of you were excited. What is the video about? What are they?

They are very fashionable. I would like to show you some pictures.

(2) Show several pictures and discuss the clothes and colours.

【设计理念：在老师与学生的交流讨论中，有意识引导学生关注模特服装的颜色，并回忆各种颜色代表的含义，为下一步列表做好准备。】

T: What is the colour of her dress? Could you tell me what green represents? What colour can you see in her clothes? What do they represent? How do you feel when you see this picture? Peaceful or powerful? Why? I guess she may be successful, why? What colour are her clothes? Does red match white very well? Red and white are a good match. Why?

Step 2 *Presentation and practice*

(1) Present a list of different colours and their meanings.

【设计理念：在研究颜色与情绪之间关系的课题之前，让学生了解各种颜色的含义，并帮助学生学会利用表格组织思路。】

T: We have talked so much about colours. Do you still remember their meanings? When we do such projects, it's a good idea to organize the information in a table. Here is a table. Can you fill in it according to your knowledge of colours? Practice (Pair work & Group work)

【设计理念：本步骤设计了多种任务，按照 list—pair work—report—group work 的任务安排，结合单词—短语—句子—篇章操练的顺序，循序渐进，层层深入，让学生自主探究，并与同桌、组员相互合作，完成预设的任务。】

(2) Talk about the picture and finish Millie's report on colours and what they represent.

【设计理念：此处教师给出五个问题的指导，帮助学生研究 part A 的图片，并提取有用的信息。pair work 的设计，让学生在列表的基础上，利用表格信息，观察图片细节，讨论并操练颜色及其含义。另外，学生们根据图片的信息，结合表格，完成 Millie 关于颜色及所代表含义的报告。】

T: Here is a picture. Look at it carefully and talk with your partner about some details. You can try to answer the following questions.

* How many people are there in the picture?
* Where is the woman?
* What is the woman wearing?
* Does she look happy?
* Do you like what she is wearing?

Now, please talk with your partner about more details, and you can use the dialogue here as a model.

(3) The structure of the sample writing and group work

【设计理念：对教材中范文的处理和结构的分析能帮助学生建立写作的框架。group work 的设计旨在使学生能独立思考，自主探究，研究老师或者同学的服装和颜色，推断人物的性格和心情，为下面的写作稍做铺垫。】

T: Millie is doing a project on the relationship between people's moods and the colours they choose to wear. Help her complete part of her report using the table here. Read the passage quickly. Can you divide the report into three parts and tell me the main idea of each part? Our teachers wear different clothes every day. Can you choose one of them and talk about his/her clothes, colours and your feelings with your group members?

Step 3 *Writing preparation*

(1) Use the two advertisements in Part B as an example to prepare some related materials for students to talk about.

【设计理念：通过让学生模仿 Millie 的颜色列表，列出广告图片中模特服装颜色所代表的含义。该部分旨在帮助学生准备写作素材，并整理思路。】

T：Your art teacher has two advertisements for you to discuss. Look at the two pictures carefully and try to make a list of colours and their meanings. What do you think of them? Are they good advertisements? Try to make some notes first.

(2) Pair work(Talk about their ideas)

【设计理念：教师提供一些表达，如：This advertisement makes me feel ... ; I like/don't like this advertisement because ... ; It is attractive/boring/exciting/funny ... 等，鼓励学生发挥想象，开拓思维。在分享交流过程中，勇于提出不同的意见，并突破思维定式，能够大胆提出不同的修改意见，而不是盲目地赞同图片中颜色的选用。】

T：Now, you can exchange your notes with your classmates, and try to find something new and interesting from others.（找两组）

Step 4 *Writing*

【设计理念：到本环节为止，教师已经从文章结构、内容和语言等方面为学生写作文做了充分的准备，也通过 pair work 让学生对所接受的知识进行了组织。写作指导重点强调学生的语篇构成及思维的开放性，鼓励学生敢于创作，力求文章有条理、有层次、表达地道。】

T：Now, choose one of the advertisements and use your notes to write a report on the relationship between the colours and the model's moods. How many paragraphs will you write?

T：(PPT 呈现表格，展示文章的基本框架) Please take out a piece of paper and write.（开始写作）

Step 5 *How to appraise a good writing*(点评作文)

【设计理念：PPT 呈现五星评分标准，给学生以直观的写作指导，有例可依，严格按照中考要求，规范写作。】

T：(利用投影展示一篇学生作文) Before checking, let us see how to

appreciate a wonderful writing.

If you write in different paragraphs, you will get a star. If your report includes all your notes, you will get a star. If your article is attractive and interesting, and you have some new and excellent ideas, you will get two stars. If you have no mistakes and your handwriting is good, you will get another star. Are you clear?

(1) Appraise a student's writing.

【设计理念:课堂批改一个学生的作文,通过教师的提问,再次向学生强调结构和语言对于一篇好作文的重要性,同时也强化学生对于五星评价标准的理解,为下面同学互评、优化自己的作文做好充分准备。在学生互评作文的环节,学生除了可以更清楚地知道如何按要求写一篇好文章外,还可以互相学习,取长补短。】

T: Let us check it together. How many paragraphs? Has he/she written all the information? Is the article very interesting? Are there any mistakes?

How about his/her handwriting? So, how many stars will she/he get?

(2) Appraise with each other and in groups.

【设计理念:在学生互评作文的环节,学生除了可以更清楚地知道如何按要求写一篇好文章,还可以互相学习,取长补短。】

T: Now, please reread your partner's article and check how many stars he/she will get.

(给学生一两分钟互评的时间)

T: How many stars does your partner get? Why?

T: This time, please read your group members' articles and choose the best one to show!

Step 5 *Conclusion*

【设计理念:情感升华,让学生能再次体会颜色与情绪的关系,热爱生活,享受生活。】

T: In our daily life, we can use different colours to change our moods.

Besides, we should try our best to make the world more colourful!

Step 6 *Homework*

【设计理念:通过认真修改自己的作文,并与同学互相讨论,学生能将本

节课所学运用到作文中去。学生还可以通过网络搜索更多信息，进而对颜色与情绪的关系有更深刻的理解，便于在实际生活运用。】

T: Your articles are really wonderful. Here is your homework:

① Read your classmates' reports to find something useful.

② Discuss with your classmates and make your own report better.

③ Surf the Internet to find more information about colours and moods.

Ⅷ Blackboard design

9A Unit 2 Colour—Task

Colours and moods

trust
calm
warm—warmth
handbag
match (*n.*) a good match
balance

Structure	
Part 1(1)	Clothes and colours.
Part 2(2 - 3)	The relationship between colours and moods.
Part 3(4)	The writer's feeling about the clothes.

Ⅸ Teaching reflection

本节课在设计时强调了 Task 课型对于本单元内容的复习与回顾，并在此基础之上进行语篇的输出训练，特别为学生准备了充分的素材和为学生提供了写作的详细指导。情境的创设、多媒体的使用、多种教学法的结合使用使得课堂环节紧凑、内容丰富、操练到位、指导规范，既激发了学生学习的兴趣，又通过小组合作探究的任务驱动，使学生积极参与课堂讨论，课堂效率高。教学内容的设计由词到句，由句到篇，层层递进，逐步深入，促进学生积极思考。任务完成以小组为单位，通过 pair work, group work 等活动，体现了“自主、合作、探究”的理念，全方位地帮助学生理解掌握本节课所学知识，并加以运用。但是在实际授课中，部分细节还有待改进与商讨。教师要掌握教学节奏，语言精练的同时要把握课堂指导的度，给学生简洁明了的指示，让学生有充分的时间思考与讨论。处理两则广告时，要引导学生在关注颜色与情绪之间关系之余，对于一些细节如阳光、广告用途等稍作考虑，并开拓思维，发挥想象。但部分同学过于追求思维的奇特，而忽略了文章写作的主旨。大多数学生能按照评价标准来完成作文，但语法错误偏多，环节设计时还应该更多地关注学生的语言输入，操练要更加丰富。

点评：

因为本课写作对象为两则广告的模特，所以老师首先播放的一段关于伦敦时装秀的视频能迅速激起学生对于颜色的兴趣，并引入话题，让他们能积极参与到课堂中来。然后师生自由对话，谈论在视频里看到的色彩，并追问学生更多关于它们的信息，创造良好的交流环境，鼓励学生勇于表达自己，为接下来的活动奠定基础，激发了学生的写作兴趣。

在本节课中，通过老师与学生的交流讨论，老师有意识引导学生关注模特服装的颜色，并回忆各种颜色代表的含义，导入生词、词组与句型，为写作积累词汇与句子，做好充分的语言材料输入，为写作输出做好准备。

本课教师通过填表格、回答问题、写提纲、归纳段落大意，再一次让学生深刻理解了范文的篇章脉络，学生的段落意识也得到进一步提升，并熟悉英语作文语句的语法思维，在学生进行正式写作时，根据自己填写的表格信息和黑板上总结的常用表达写作。写完以后学生互相批改作文，并根据表格里的评分标准打分。这样可以让学生在学习好作文的亮点和表达以及拓宽思路的同时，发现自己写作时的不足，提高自批自改的能力。

但是在处理写作课时教师注重了说、读、写之间的内在联系，也可以适当加入听力训练。建议应加强课堂的趣味性，可采用游戏、竞猜、竞争等多种形式，去激发学生的积极性，培养学生竞争与合作的精神。另外段落写作的方式主要包括句子扩展、连词的运用与句子衔接等，教师如何有效地激发学生的兴趣，让学生自主感受、总结写作方式，利用多种方式有效地讲授段落写作的方法以及课堂升华部分还可以再改进。